Sweet SUCCESS

A Simple Recipe to Turn Your Passion into Profit

CANDACE NELSON

HarperCollins
Leadership

An Imprint of HarperCollins

Published by HarperCollins Leadership, an imprint of HarperCollins Focus LLC.

Any internet addresses, phone numbers, or company or product information printed in this book are offered as a resource and are not intended in any way to be or to imply an endorsement by HarperCollins Leadership, nor does HarperCollins Leadership vouch for the existence, content, or services of these sites, phone numbers, companies, or products beyond the life of this book.

This book is written as a source of information only. The information contained in this book should by no means be considered a substitute for the advice, decisions, or judgment of the reader's professional or financial advisors. All efforts have been made to ensure the accuracy of the information contained in this book as of the date published. The author and the publisher expressly disclaim responsibility for any adverse effects arising from the use or application of the information contained herein.

Book design by Aubrey Khan, Neuwirth & Associates, Inc.

ISBN 978-1-4002-3153-9 (eBook)
ISBN 978-1-4002-3150-8 (HC)

Library of Congress Control Number: 2022943561

Printed in the United States of America
22 23 24 25 26 LSC 10 9 8 7 6 5 4 3 2 1

TO CHARLIE AND HARRY:

Do not go where the path may lead, go instead where there is no path and leave a trail.
—Ralph Waldo Emerson

CONTENTS

Part Three

BUILD IT! CHANNEL YOUR MULTITASKING OPERATOR

Part Four

PROTECT IT! BE PREPARED TO LEAD, DEFEND, AND PLAN FOR THE FUTURE

Introduction
PREHEAT YOUR IDEA

love the feeling of possibility that comes with starting something new. Whether it's creating a modern take on a classic recipe or dreaming up an innovative new venture with loads of potential, a fresh start lights me up. When someone tells me they have a new idea, I'm all in, ready to roll up my sleeves and figure out how to help make it a reality. If a friend is pondering leaving their stale, yet stable, career to pursue a passion, I'm basically writing their resignation letter before they've fully made up their mind.

This is because I was once at a pivotal moment myself, and entrepreneurship catapulted me down a new path I would have never thought possible. I now know, firsthand, the immeasurable joy that comes from pushing past a confusing crossroads and discovering what you were born to do. Today, I can speak to the pride and confidence that comes from taking what was once just an inkling and boldly bringing it to life.

I turned my passion into profit by starting small—like, palm-of-your-hand small. It began with a cupcake and grew into an empire. These days, I hear from so many people who want to start their own business too. They are dreamers who want to make their mark on the world and carve out a piece of the economy that is all their own, yet they don't know how to begin. Without a road map, the idea of starting a business for the first time seems unattainable, so instead they hit the pause button on their dreams. Well, failure to launch no more! I'm here to tell you that the path to entrepreneurship is yours for the taking. Sure, it's intimidating when founders are glamorized as the subject of feature films and steal the spotlight on hit shows like *Shark Tank*; they may even seem mystical, when billion-dollar start-ups are referred to as "unicorns." It can be easy to forget that entrepreneurs are just regular people. Speaking as one of them, I won't sugarcoat it. Building a business from scratch is not for the faint of heart. But I do believe that anyone can be an entrepreneur—all it takes is a proper plan and the right attitude.

This book is about just that—gathering the ingredients to start baking the business of your dreams.

One of the reasons I felt compelled to write this book is to dispel the myth that entrepreneurs have something that the rest of us don't. One of the most valuable lessons I've learned is that you don't need an exceptional IQ to create something exceptional. Believe me, I wasn't exactly top of my class in high school.

When I was growing up, my family moved every few years, including internationally, for my father's job as general counsel for an American multinational corporation. I know it may sound exciting to travel the world as a child. And as an adult, I can now appreciate the deeply diverse cultural experiences I encountered at such a young age. But moving often during my school years was tough. As a lanky thirteen-year-old American girl living in Indonesia, I longed desperately for a sense of home and belonging.

It wasn't much better when I was sent back to the United States to attend a rigorous boarding school. I was the youngest in my class and my family was still on the other side of the globe. A comforting phone call home was hard to come by: There was only one pay phone in my dorm, and between the time difference and poor international connection fraught with static, calls to my family were often dropped.

Despite the school's accolades and reputation for academic excellence, the learning environment was all wrong for me. The school days were tightly structured, which clashed with my creativity. The emphasis on high achievement in a traditional curriculum made it difficult for me to find success, and I wandered in search of other interests. I refocused my efforts on fun: finding a ride to the next Phish concert and playing pranks on my dormmates instead of getting good grades. Needless to say, I received my fair share of detention for my wayward ways.

I suppose my reputation for being middle of the road during high school stuck around because at an alumni event a few years back, a former classmate approached me with a decent amount of disbelief while congratulating me on my success with Sprinkles. Sure, I was a little offended, but after years in the public eye I've learned not to take things personally. Mediocre classmate turns her life around and makes something of herself? I guess all the misplaced creativity, resourcefulness, and rebelliousness that sent me to detention are the building blocks for what have made me a successful entrepreneur.

The road to entrepreneurship will look different for everyone, but the ingredient connecting all founders is a great idea that we can't stop obsessing over until we put it into action. Regardless of how you got here, or the type of business you want to create, I can help you. In this book, I will be your mentor, guiding you from career crossroads to new business launch. I will empower you by giving you the actionable tools and information you need to listen confidently to your inner voice and take your big idea from passion project to business venture, first by dreaming it, then packaging and building it, and finally, protecting it.

But sometimes, even with all the planning in the world, you still won't feel ready. Making the leap to entrepreneurship is ultimately about taking the first step, then the next. I call it following the bread crumbs. I wrote this book to encourage you to go for it, so think of this as your first crumb.

Now, let's get cooking!

Part One
DREAM IT!

How to Be a Founder

I n a start-up company there is no hierarchy, very little in terms of structure and job descriptions, and, frankly, lots to do and not enough people to do it. As a new founder, you will be short on time and even more
so on money. You will have to be scrappy and wear many hats that would
normally be worn by an entire management team at a more established
company. At Sprinkles, among other roles, I created the product and
brand story, hired and trained employees, evaluated new locations,
crafted PR campaigns, and represented the brand on TV around the
world. Oh yeah, I was also in charge of taking out the trash at night.

Assuming responsibility for all these functions as a founder is exhausting and exhilarating. In fact, there is literally no good reason why
anyone would want to go out and build something that didn't exist

before, only to risk money, reputation, and a whole lot of sleep to execute something that everyone thinks is a terrible idea. So how and why do you do it? Because you have a dream you just can't shake until it becomes a reality. And you realize that no one is going to make that happen except you.

When you're a founder, you are a pie-in-the-sky, head-in-the-clouds dreamer. You see change where others see more of the same. You are the Walt to Disney Studios, the Mrs. Fields to the chocolate chip cookie, and the Steve Jobs to that phone you're holding in your hand.

In this section, we are going to dream together. I will share those early days when Sprinkles was just a spark of an idea in my mind, and I will guide you through the emotional preparation and mental maneuvering to get you to that place where you are ready to take the leap. So, hold on to (all of) your hats, my friends, and let's start dreaming big!

Step One

GATHER THE ESSENTIALS

Use passion and purpose to propel you.

Assembling the tools and ingredients for any recipe before you begin is good baking technique. Known in professional kitchens as mise en place, this practice helps ensure that nothing is accidentally forgotten in the baking process. After many years in the kitchen, mise en place is now instinctive for me, but when I first began baking, my methods were much more haphazard. I often forgot ingredients, noticing only once it was too late. In retrospect, my mishaps in the kitchen mirrored the scattered way that I moved from place to place growing up. As a child living overseas, it turns out the key missing ingredient for me was a sense of home.

I had a perpetual longing for life back in the States. Back then, international phone calls were extremely expensive and required parental permission. When I wrote and mailed letters to my pen pals back home, it would take two weeks for the letters to reach them. To alleviate my homesickness more quickly, I turned to the treats I loved—American desserts like chocolate chip cookies, Rice Krispies Treats, and frosted cupcakes. In Indonesia, there were no bakeries offering such "exotic" delicacies, so I had to learn to make them myself. I spent hours in the kitchen alongside my mom and her well-worn copy of *Joy of Cooking* baking the confections I craved. I became mesmerized by the science and art of baking, and I loved the way every recipe felt like home. I found comfort and a certain measure of control in baking (well, except when the Indonesian humidity turned my meringue to mush). It was a constant in my ever-changing environment and gave me something in return: passion.

That same passion became the foundation for Sprinkles and was vital to its success. In recent years, some experts argue that having personal passion for what you do is overhyped. They say that at the end of the day, a successful business is about customer satisfaction, not fulfilling your own passion. That's why some business pundits recommend a more pragmatic approach of finding an unmet consumer need (also known as *whitespace* in investor circles) and solving a problem over something as risky as pursuing a passion. While I agree that you should establish whether there is a market for your product, I don't think you should analyze the competitive landscape without regard for personal interests. The ability to combine one's passion with an unmet consumer need is the ultimate sweet spot for any new business.

Growing up, I was the quintessential "well-rounded" kid. It seemed like a good thing until college graduation; then it just felt like a euphemism for *confused*. Unlike my law school–bound or premed friends, I had absolutely no clue what I was going to do with my life. So, I did what most people without a clear career path do: just get a job. Though I was a planner, I wasn't so sure about what I was planning to do exactly. I desperately wanted to identify and own "my thing." Being a jack-of-all-trades felt like a liability when everyone seemed to have crystal clear goals. Yet, I felt paralyzed by indecision. (Spoiler alert: If you like doing multiple things and don't have a singular focus, you might just make an ideal entrepreneur!)

I was recruited into an investment banking analyst program in San Francisco right out of school. Since I had spent my formative years on the East Coast, there's probably something romantic to say about going out west to explore new frontiers and seek golden opportunities. But honestly, I was looking to lock down any job that put me on a clear career path in a respected field and paid a salary that covered my rent.

I joined a firm that helped companies raise capital through initial public offerings (IPOs) and consulted on financial transactions like mergers and acquisitions (M&A). Let me be clear: I had never even taken an accounting course. In fact, my liberal arts college idealistically refused to offer one! I was a fish out of water from day one, but it was a prestigious job where I hoped to build a solid business foundation—a smart first step into the professional world, I thought. It felt like the "right" choice to make. But crunching numbers into the wee hours of the night was draining my soul instead of feeding it. I was anxious all the time, lived in fear of my bosses, and developed a pit in my stomach every time a project landed on my desk on Friday at 5 p.m.—which happened most Fridays. Don't get me wrong, I enjoyed the camaraderie and connection with my coworkers, but our bonds were mostly formed over a shared sense of anxiety, fear, and stress. We were like the last handful of competitors on the TV show *Survivor*, forming alliances to endure and outlast.

Though it was grueling much of the time, the perks were huge. I'm not talking about vacation time, benefits, or cold brew on tap. I'm referring to the dinners. The deal celebrations, or "closing dinners," exposed me to some of the best restaurants in the world.

Food has always been *everything* in my family. From the classic American desserts I habitually baked with my mom, to frequent outings in the Singapore market stalls to feast on noodles and chile crab, our enthusiasm for food was a constant no matter where we relocated. Even our vacations were about food. A family trip to France was a thinly veiled excuse to sample crêpes, meringues, and *pains au chocolat*.

I couldn't believe my luck that I'd landed a job out of college that allowed me to dine regularly at high-end bistros such as The French Laundry, Boulevard, and Jardinière. These experiences awakened my deeply rooted familial appreciation for good food and a thirst for more knowledge around the dishes themselves. I began fangirling chefs, re-searching farms, and appreciating the importance of a well-sourced in-gredient from the right purveyor. I became a regular at the Ferry Plaza Farmers Market, walking around smelling coffee, tasting chocolates, and devouring freshly baked goods. I started to get the inkling that this wasn't just a hobby.

You have to remember that this was San Francisco in 1998. While I was eating my way through the upper echelons of the city's eateries, I also had a front-row seat to a bubbling tech and dot-com boom. People were jumping ship from traditional jobs and becoming millionaires over-night through stock options at fast-rising internet companies. California was experiencing its second gold rush, and I wanted in on this exciting adventure. I left my financial firm and accepted a job at a start-up called Snap.com (no, not Snapchat!). Snap.com was a web portal and its mis-sion was to become the new Yahoo! The expense accounts, and my dining adventures, continued despite the career shift. It was what they called "a frothy time." One team-building trip meant going to Napa to eat at Michael Chiarello's Tra Vigne and ride hot-air balloons. If this was the life of a professional, maybe I could get used to it.

Unfortunately, I didn't have much of a chance. In March 2000 the dot-com bubble peaked and within a year the market had crashed. High-flying internet companies were folding in record numbers, resulting in an estimated $5 trillion worth of stock market value being wiped out. More pressingly, I found myself out of a job.

I wasn't alone. The exodus from San Francisco was so extreme that there was a six-week wait for a U-Haul truck. I was paralyzed with inde-cision, frustrated that I had once again found myself at a career cross-roads when all my peers seemingly had their lives together. Friends were heading back to school to get their master's degree or switching gears to work for nonprofits. Here I was, just as directionless as when I started, feeling as if I were being left behind while everyone powered on without me. The professional world had spit me right back out in the same place it found me, confused.

With nowhere to go and no plan in place, I slipped into a mild depres-sion. My days were dictated by *TV Guide*, punctuated by important meetings with Oprah Winfrey and Martha Stewart. These shows were my refuge and inspiration—the recipes and crafts that Martha had built into an industrial complex, and the noteworthy guests Oprah interviewed, wormed their way into my subconscious.

How could they not? Overnight, I went from grinding sixteen hours a day nonstop to marking the passage of time by reruns. I was paralyzed, on my couch, in the prime of my life, applying for jobs I had no interest in taking. I remember one interview I thought went totally sideways, until they called me for a second round. Instead of being pleasantly surprised, I couldn't even bring myself to go back; my heart wasn't in it even though I wanted it to be. No jobs, fields, or industries compelled me, and working for myself felt way out of reach. I couldn't go home to live with my parents—they were in Bangkok. So I considered my options.

Although I had been immersed in a world of successful entrepreneurship, it felt like an inaccessible path for me. The entrepreneurs I witnessed were engineers and technical savants building Silicon Valley and changing the world. Sure, I dreamed of being an entrepreneur, but without a technical skill set, I couldn't see myself as one. And knowing how to discern different cacao contents in chocolate didn't seem like it would fly with investors.

Besides, I didn't want to code; I wanted to play. So I did.

Whether it was all that Martha Stewart, the endless stretches of time on my hands, or my insatiable sweet tooth, I started to spend some serious time in the kitchen. I got messy with fondant and piped with buttercream. I morphed flour and eggs into cookies and cakes. I felt a sense of joy and possibility while I baked and frosted, stacked and molded. The irony is that while I was doing something fun without any expectation, I was rewarded with the vision to spot an amazing opportunity.

PICK YOUR PASSION

It's entirely possible to have more than one passion in your life. In fact, the more, the better! But not every passion translates to business success. Here are three things to keep in mind when you're considering transforming a passion into a business:

1. **Passion often comes with some industry expertise.** When I had the idea to open a first-of-its-kind cupcake bakery, I was immersed in the baking world: I lived, breathed, shopped, and read everything baking. What better place to look around and see what the market is missing but from the vantage point of an expert?

2. **Passion opens doors.** When starting a business, you don't just need to attract throngs of customers; you need a network of investors, suppliers, vendors, and supporters. With earnest passion in your pocket, other people in your sphere will fall under your spell. Passion is contagious, and the more you have, the faster it will spread to the right people to help make your idea happen.

3. **Passion keeps you in business.** It's so hard to start a company, let alone keep one going year after year. If you don't have a fire in your belly, the numerous obstacles that you encounter are more likely to send you running the other way. Passion is fuel for the determination you need to see your idea through.

> **If you're starting something on your own, you better have a passion for it, because this is hard work.**
> —*Sallie Krawcheck, Founder of Ellevest*

When I first considered pursuing my passion as a profession, I wasn't convinced it was the right move or if I would even like it. I knew I loved to bake as a hobby out of my kitchen for friends and family, but how could I be sure I would enjoy it when it became a daily grind? I enrolled in a highly respected pastry school in San Francisco called Tante Marie's. It was the only way to quell the uncertainty that was plaguing me.

After six months, I found the answer I'd hoped for: I loved it. I took pleasure in working with my hands—the tactile quality of kneading flour and sugar and butter. I cherished creating something that people could consume and enjoy. I especially appreciated that the results were tangible and immediately gratifying, such a contrast to the hours I'd previously spent in front of a computer screen modeling hypothetical financial scenarios. I loved the challenge of balancing art and science with delicious, beautiful creations such as luscious layer cakes and delicate pastry. I felt focused and creative, energized yet relaxed. Hours would go by, yet it felt like an instant. I had finally found *my thing.*

You might be wondering where to go from here if you don't have a "thing." Trust me, I was right there with you. My copy of *What Color Is Your Parachute?* was worn thin and I even invested in expensive career aptitude testing hoping some calling would surface. But just because you haven't identified a personal passion doesn't mean you don't have one. One approach for uncovering what drives you is to consider your flow. Flow, a concept introduced by psychologist Mihaly Csikszentmihalyi in the seventies, is an optimal state of heightened focus and complete immersion in an activity. You may have heard athletes refer to it as being "in the zone." When you are in your flow, you are so engaged in doing something that you enjoy, or are passionate about, that you can easily lose track of time. I had experienced this expansive state of flow while baking in my kitchen.

Think back to a time when you were doing something you were passionate about. What was it? Did you feel you were in a state of flow?

ADD PURPOSE TO MAKE IT SHINE

You can't have passion without purpose. If passion is the chocolate, then purpose is the cream—it emulsifies and brings everything together into one glossy, luscious ganache. Purpose is a brand's reason for being, yes, even before profit. It can help establish an emotional connection with the customer as well as employees, creating a strong community that resonates with your values and aligns with your purpose. So often companies launch without a purpose and end up falling flat with nothing emotionally resonant to offer beyond the product itself. Having heart is what steers a business through inevitable challenges. At Sprinkles, my purpose wasn't to sling cupcakes; I wanted to bring universal joy to my community and beyond. Look, the cupcakes were *really* good, but the premium product isn't what brought people into the store multiple times a week. It was the delight and nostalgia for simpler, happy moments that built true brand loyalty.

Providing a connection point in a divided world is what captivated our customers. I heard tales of entertainment executives kicking off meetings by talking about everyone's favorite Sprinkles flavors. It makes total sense to me. What better way to get on the same page for a business meeting than to connect over a universal, delicious topic of conversation? In this way, a Sprinkles Cupcake is not just a tasty treat—it represents something bigger: a place where everyone can get along. I wanted to strengthen the bond among friends, coworkers, and generations over a small piece of cake. This higher goal is what gives meaning to my work every day. It's understandable—I had started Sprinkles amid my own personal career frustration and a forever changed nation.

Three and a half years before I first opened Sprinkles' doors, 9/11 happened. Most everyone knows exactly where they were when they heard the news. I was sitting in an airport in the south of France on the last leg of my honeymoon, when reports of something major happening in New York began to dominate the TV screens. All my carefree, euphoric vacation feelings immediately faded as my new husband, Charles, and I strained to see television journalists covering the attack—entirely in French. My happy newlywed daze was slowly replaced by fear and a sinking sensation of a dark unknown. For months, and even years, it colored my outlook. I've always been an optimist, but during this period, most things seemed so meaningless. What was I doing with my life? I was unfulfilled by my work, and knew I needed to do something that felt impactful. After the most anxious flight I've ever taken to the East Coast, and one cross-country drive back to San Francisco, we were home. The following year, I enrolled in pastry school. I was on a quest for a small piece of tangible joy that I could deliver back to the world, and I knew it involved three things: sugar, flour, and butter.

That feeling guided me both in the beginning and as Sprinkles scaled. In a turbulent world, I wanted to offer comfort through cake. And, in an environment that felt divisive and fractured, I felt moved to build a business whose mission was to connect and unify.

FOOD FOR THOUGHT

In order to find your passion and purpose, ask yourself these questions:

What is a topic you could talk about for hours or that your friends consider you an expert on?

What do you do to have fun? Or what did you love to do as a child?

What impact do you want to make on the world?

What do you want to achieve in your life?

Step Two

PREP YOUR MINDSET

*Cultivate confidence, befriend failure,
and reject imposter syndrome.*

I f entrepreneurship boils down to one thing, it's betting on yourself. As unsure as the entrepreneurial path can be, working for someone else is no less risky. For instance, during the first few months of the pandemic, 22 million workers lost their jobs. But, even when we are not in crisis, or when the world is not upside down, you should never put all your eggs in one basket—unless it's your own.

FIND YOUR CONFIDENCE

I did just that, and not only because I'm a baker. I was beyond scared of leaving the corporate world to set out on my dicey cupcake idea, but what frightened me even more was what would happen if I stayed in a cubicle. I'll never forget the wisdom an early Sprinkles customer shared with me: "In a company it just takes one person to lose your job—your boss. When you own a business, you are no longer at the whim of just one person." Think about that: As a business owner, the only way you'll be "fired" is if all your customers put you out of a job. I would take those odds any day.

There was so much I didn't know when I started Sprinkles—I didn't have experience making cupcakes at scale, I had never run a retail shop before, and I had no clue about marketing or operations. In spite of my fears, the one thing I was sure of was that I could count on myself.

Often, circumstances in life may force you to find your strength. Having spent most of my childhood in Southeast Asia, with a few years of elementary school in the Midwest and then boarding school in New England, I was forced to regularly make new friends and find my community. Having to walk into new classrooms and seek out new lunch tables all the time was scary and exhausting. Other kids got to go to school with the same class their whole lives, but my best friends turned into pen pals in a matter of a year. On TV, I watched Blair, Tootie, Natalie, and Jo all grow up with each other on *The Facts of Life*, and all I wanted was to be like them. Looking back, I realize this was an exercise in resilience, and I can now see how it's shaped my adult self. Starting over and building from the ground up became a survival skill and a muscle I strengthened over time.

Many elements go into building your overall confidence. For aspiring entrepreneurs, it's important to tap into your own past resilience to feel confident in facing future obstacles. Unfortunately, the hits will keep coming between crests of success. When was the last time you decided to change a habit, initiate a difficult conversation, or stand up and speak publicly? These are the building blocks to the type of confidence you need to start a business. Conversely, when was the last time you had your heart broken, didn't get the job, had your performance criticized, or lost your train of thought in an interview? No doubt, you survived! This, too, is how you build the confidence necessary to commit to your idea.

When you have the ability to fail, get up, and keep going, then you know you're ready to start the journey of becoming an entrepreneur.

Once you start to feel your confidence come alive, it's time to channel it in a way that can set you up for success.

PUT THAT PERSPECTIVE INTO PRACTICE

Before you can throw on your best apron and get your hands dirty, it's important to do a little prep work. Buoyant with your new confidence, pick one or two of these exercises to test the waters outside your comfort zone.

- **Put yourself in a new position.** This doesn't need to be a grand gesture to yourself. Change is hard, even to our own daily routines. Afraid of public speaking? Give a small toast at the next birthday dinner you attend. Don't love attending events or parties without a wingman? Go solo next time. For me, my childhood involved stepping into unknown situations all the time, but by continually showing up for new and nerve-wracking experiences on my own I ultimately built my bravery. Every time you put yourself in an unknown or challenging situation you have an opportunity to learn, grow, and build your confidence around something you never thought you could do. The goal is not for fear to disappear completely, but for it to lose its lock on you. You might surprise yourself how well you rise to the challenge and how easy it becomes.
- **Commit to starting before you're ready.** Call it a self-fulfilling prophecy if that sounds a little more magical. The point is to believe it before you see it. And I mean you *really* need to believe it. If you don't believe in it, then how will anyone else? Long before I opened Sprinkles, I blabbed to everyone I knew that I was opening a cupcake shop. It was still unclear if that would ever become a possibility. I was internally motivated but was also adding an external motivation to keep me honest. Whenever I saw a friend, they would ask me how it was going. It would have been embarrassing to admit that I'd given up. I prided myself on being a person who did what they said they

were going to do. I also found that the more I said it out loud to another person, the more real it felt, and the more deeply I believed it would happen.

- **Take a leap.** Talk is so critical in the beginning, but at some point, it becomes cheap without the action to back it up. I loved to bake and always dreamed of opening my own bakery, but it wasn't until I enrolled not in business school but a professional pastry program that I had to do the work behind the dream. Eventually, you'll have to put your money, hands, and brains where your mouth is. Sometimes it takes a few false starts to build up the courage to take that leap. But once you do, you're never going back.

- **Go one step at a time.** Entrepreneurs certainly have heady goals, but if I had set off to build a national brand on day one, I would have fizzled out and given up. Take wedding cakes, for example. They involve so many steps—from baking, cooling, and torting the cakes to making and tinting the buttercream, cooking the fillings, and molding all the decorations. This is why master cake makers break up these steps over a matter of days. Sometimes cakes are made so far in advance that they are frozen and then thawed to allow time to create all the other components. The same goes for building a business; you need to go step by step. Breaking that lofty idea down into manageable steps is what makes those larger-scale goals attainable.

TAME IMPOSTER SYNDROME

I believe the path to self-made success is available to anyone. If you don't believe you can do this, particularly if you are a woman, know that you are not alone. A 2019 article by NatWest Group claimed nearly 60 percent of women delay starting a business because of "imposter syndrome," a feeling commonly experienced by high-achieving people. If you've felt it, you recognize that hard-to-shake feeling of being a fraud, accompanied by deep shame and fear that you will be found out. Women, in particular, tend to think that they're not ready. They feel unprepared. They believe they need a little more time to proof.

I felt this way too. When I decided to start Sprinkles, I hadn't followed the typical path out of pastry school, toiling in the industry for years or staging under famous chefs. I hadn't even worked in a bakery. Who was I to think I could compete in the industry?

What's worse is that imposter syndrome can still nag at you long after you reach your goals. In the early days of Sprinkles, during any rare moment of downtime I would devour self-help and business books. At one point, my husband and business partner, Charles, walked in to see me reading Jack Canfield's *The Success Principles*. The book's promise? Get ready to transform yourself for success. Charles started laughing and reminded me that my business had a line around the block and that I didn't need that book. "Easy for you to say!" I grumbled under my breath, and I kept on reading. But that's imposter syndrome: Even though Charles was right, and despite all the hard work and now insatiable demand for my cupcakes, I still felt unworthy.

There are a few ways to tame imposter syndrome.

1. **Fake it until you make it!** Corny, I know, but this advice is enduring for good reason: It works. This mantra served me well all those years that I was walking into new school lunchrooms, and it still serves me in times of self-doubt today.

2. **Celebrate your wins.** Every time you acknowledge an accomplishment, you build that belief in yourself a little bit more.

3. **Remember you're not alone.** In fact, you are in great company. So many notables—from Sheryl Sandberg to Howard Schultz to Lady Gaga—have admitted to feeling imposter syndrome.

To this day, I still feel a pang of insecurity when someone from the food industry asks who I apprenticed with, since my resume lacks that credential. But that pang is tempered by what I know now: Far more important than a fancy education is that fearless first step.

MAKE FRIENDS WITH FAILURE

Sometimes not getting what you want—or what you believe you want—is exactly what you need to move ahead. I believe anyone can build a thriving business with the right mindset and guidance, but I also believe that you will have to embrace your stumbles, fumbles, and mistakes.

One of my first important personal appearances after launching Sprinkles was when Maria Shriver asked me to be on a panel at her Women's Conference. She was the first lady of California at the time and was using her platform (as she still actively does) to support and inspire women. The event was a big deal, packed with famous women, and I was thrilled and honored to be included in the lineup. Not to mention the perks included car service, hair and makeup, a great swag bag from all the sponsors, and a walk on the red carpet. Winning! Our panel presented to a packed room for forty-five minutes and then it was time for Q&A. After a few audience members had asked their questions, a woman stood up and began asking a question that was so long and incomprehensible that I actually started to tune out. There was no way it was a question for me. For one thing, the woman had used some jargon that I had never heard before. Beyond that, I was sitting among women with much more impressive resumes—including Danica Patrick, a professional race car driver! The sound of my name broke through my daze and suddenly, every eyeball in that room was staring at me, awaiting an answer. I went from basking in the glow of a panel well done to burning with embarrassment. I tried to muddle my way through an answer to a question I hadn't understood or even fully heard. I can't even remember what I said, but it wasn't pretty or vaguely authoritative. Just like that, my triumphant day had turned into a big fat fail. I thought, *Who was I to be an authority on a panel when I couldn't even understand the business terminology that people were using?* I could have steered clear of public appearances after my deer-in-headlights moment on stage at the Women's Conference. I certainly wanted to. All of a sudden, the unpredictability of live questions in a Q&A format felt like a potential landmine! Instead, I realized a valuable lesson that has served me well for the countless podcasts, firesides, and personal appearances I have done since then: the power of honesty. "I don't know," "I'm not sure I understand," and "I haven't thought about that. Let me get back to you" are perfectly acceptable responses, and I pull them out regularly in similar situations. Sure, it sounds vulnerable to admit to not having all the answers, but it doesn't mean you're a fraud. It simply means you're human. I could have just owned up to not understanding that audience member's question. I could have asked her to rephrase it or maybe even give her the spotlight and ask her to educate me on the concept she was asking about. We all have things to learn from each other. Owning up to failure is a universal experience that everyone can relate to. What will show the world you're a pro is how well you deal with it.

Granted, our culture is not very forgiving when it comes to failure, leading many of us to try to avoid it at all costs. But when you spend all your time dodging failure, you will rarely find success. In fact, constructive failure is one of the keys to entrepreneurship. Seems a bit counterintuitive, but as this eloquent observation (often attributed to Winston Churchill) says, "Success is stumbling from failure to failure with no loss of enthusiasm." This is easier said than done. For all you perfectionists out there who can't imagine showing your messy selves to the world, allow me to introduce you to my two favorite *FAIL* acronyms:

1. **F**irst **A**ttempt **I**n **L**earning
2. **F**orever **A**cquiring **I**mportant **L**essons

When I think of failure, I try to channel my inner toddler. Have you ever watched them learn to walk? I used to scurry after my son Charlie when he was taking his first steps, my arms outstretched to catch him as he would inevitably fall backward. Yet, undeterred, he always got back up and doggedly pushed on. If you find yourself overly frustrated with falling backward, take a moment to reconnect with your inner toddler. With any new challenge, there will always be a period of wobbling and stumbling. Harnessing that childlike determination will keep you moving forward, one step at a time.

Sometimes it can even be a relief to fail. When your greatest fear comes true, it releases you from the anticipation, grounding you in the reality that your fear was greater than the event itself. Failure is fear realized. Once it's out of your mind and staring you in the face, it's a lot less scary; small, even. Failures make your fear much easier to conquer and give you the confidence to face it again—which is exactly what you need to grow.

When the internet bubble burst, I was at a career crossroads, but I ultimately realized that this was an opportunity to figure out what I really wanted to do with my life. My worst-case scenario of losing my job without a backup plan had played out, and I was still standing. With nothing left to lose, there was nowhere to go but up. Instead of scrambling to settle for another job that didn't fulfill me, I decided to take a risk and live on my meager savings until my next move revealed itself.

It was tempting to follow the pack and go to business school, just like my college friends and former colleagues. But, for the first time since graduating, I wasn't envious of my peers taking traditional roads well worn. Out of college, I had chosen the "practical" job, and it left me unfulfilled. Clearly, something needed to change, and I knew it needed to happen before I found myself stuck too far down a career path I resented. In the investment banking world, we used to talk about the "golden handcuffs": If you didn't get out early enough, eventually you couldn't, because you were earning so much money that any career move would result in a drastically diminished lifestyle.

When I stopped looking for jobs I didn't want, I began seeing possibilities that I did. A few people I knew had started companies—a yoga line, a contemporary bag company, a tabletop shop. These weren't the tech execs I'd see during my dot-com days, but friends who were launching small businesses or stores. This was a type of entrepreneurship I could get my head around. But how could I reach point B when point A was my couch? Today we call this "compare and despair." Have you ever scrolled through someone's Instagram feed and compared their seemingly picture-perfect life to your messy reality? It can make you want to drop your phone into the bathtub, but it can also be a kick in the pants to take action. I made a conscious decision to use it as motivation.

I wanted to break out of my circumstances and do something bigger than I had ever done—on my own terms—but this major move was going to require a totally different mindset. I had always prided myself on pursuing pragmatic, realistic plans. I always felt compelled to make the "right" choice. But once I released myself from the idea that there were right and wrong paths, I opened the floodgates for big, unwieldy dreams.

And so, while others followed their traditional, safe professional trajectories with graduate degrees, I made a slightly different investment in my education. I went off to pastry school and set out to get my "cupcake MBA."

Go ahead: Make your eyes bigger than your stomach! Forget that advice you got as a kid about not doing that—instead, pile your plate high with big dreams! When I allowed myself to dream the biggest, most audacious dreams I could think of—writing a bestselling cookbook (crazy!), being on the Food Network (even crazier!)—my pulse quickened, but I felt indomitable. Bulletproof.

FOOD FOR THOUGHT

So much of starting a business is the mindset. Do you have the right ingredients? Here are some important questions you'll need to consider.

Do you believe in yourself and your ability to tackle new challenges? Or do you need to build that confidence through practice?

Are you ready to embrace a growth mindset? Think of a time when you failed miserably: Did you see it as a learning opportunity?

Do you believe you are worthy of success? If not, are you willing to do the work to get past that limiting belief?

Do your dreams light you up? Or can you push yourself to dream bigger?

Step Three

ADD YOUR SECRET INGREDIENT

The world needs your perspective.

After graduating from pastry school, I put all my energy and new-found skills into elegant cake creations. I sourced the finest ingredients, baked out of my own kitchen for most of the day (and night), and hand-delivered each elaborate delicacy. Picture a frantic young baker balancing giant, multi-tiered cakes up the notoriously steep hills of San Francisco. In retrospect, it was a comical, almost cartoonish sight. But at the time, I found it difficult to laugh at my distress, as I was quite literally sweating confectioners' sugar. So I enlisted the help of my husband, Charles, who was sweet enough to play the role of a lifetime: a human cake stand. And even with his expert, steady hand protecting the bakery boxes from every bump along the way, it was still punishing for both of us. I would scale those precipitous hills and cringe as I heard the gut-wrenching thumps of decorations falling off my cakes.

It quickly became clear that this was not a sustainable service. Sure, I loved baking, but these cakes were slowly killing me. Plus, it was dawning on me that people don't often buy a whole cake. Sure, the holidays are a time of celebration, but for the rest of the calendar year, a special-occasion cake is reserved for, well, a rare special occasion.

My left brain started kicking in again . . . hard. I wanted to make something people could enjoy every day. It needed to be simple to create and even easier to love. The wheels started turning. What could I create that would still be special, yet baked fresh and consumed daily?

If you planned or attended a wedding in the early aughts, you know that cupcakes were becoming quite a trend on the wedding scene. These little paper-wrapped cakes, once reserved for kids' birthday parties, were now gracing the pages of *Martha Stewart Weddings* magazine as an elevated guest experience. As a recent bride, I had personally opted for the traditional wedding cake but was definitely tempted by the then-trendy cupcake tower. The appeal of a cupcake was so clear. Everyone could eat their own cake, in their favorite flavor—fork free! At a wedding, you could even take them onto the dance floor. Portable, personalized, and pretty: the cupcake.

Historically, cupcakes were an afterthought, a way to make use of excess cake batter and frosting. And, aside from the wedding scene, cupcakes were still treated as kids' fare—basic supermarket stuff with sad plastic picks as decoration. (By the way, whose idea was it to make a sharp plastic pick a decorative norm for small children?!) They were never very delicious either. Made with shortening-laden frostings and waxy, garishly colored sprinkles, cupcakes never tasted as good as you wanted them to be.

It couldn't have been more obvious: The humble cupcake needed a makeover. The market was ready for cupcakes, but they needed a proper upgrade. Everything about them needed a face-lift; the flavors, ingredients, and look of the cupcake all needed to be elevated. I envisioned a sophisticated cupcake that appealed to adults but still felt playful enough to keep the kids clamoring.

How would that look? Could a cupcake ever be *sophisticated*? Would it work to use the same incredible ingredients I used for my decorative cakes? What if I made cupcakes so special that they could stand on their own as single-serving occasion cakes?

When interviewing founders seeking investment money, legendary entrepreneur turned venture capitalist Peter Thiel always asks, "What important truth do very few people agree with you on?" For me, my belief that the world needed luxury cupcakes was exactly the truth that only I could see. I knew this to be true based on a distinctive mix of passion for what I was doing, my understanding of the bakery landscape, and a frustration at what was lacking. But almost no one (except Charles) agreed with me! I had discovered my secret ingredient, that insight that only I possessed based on my unique position and experiences.

WHAT IS YOUR UNIQUE INSIGHT?

V enture capitalist Ben Horowitz calls this "an earned secret." What do you see that other people don't? What knowledge do you hold that shapes your lens of the world? What's your insider advantage?

For Alli Webb, it was understanding that most of the services hair salons offered could be cut. A decade ago, no one was jumping at opportunities in the legacy salon industry. While most entrepreneurs would identify the space as well-trod territory, Webb had worked in salons for years and saw an opportunity to reinvent an antiquated model. Sure, traditional salons were working just fine, but Webb's new Drybar addressed something they could not readily offer: quick, inexpensive blowouts at volume. Webb understood a customer's pain point—the desire to feel the confidence that comes with a salon-quality blowout more than a few times a year—and delivered a new kind

of business. Drybar became a sensation because it didn't necessarily compete with full-service salons. Rather, it comple-
mented their offerings by focusing on one popular service and
making it fast, affordable, and accessible.

Elevating and spotlighting the potential in a cupcake made complete sense to me. My childhood spent overseas introduced me to the
idea of "doing one thing and doing it well." America was the land of the
supermarket, but in many countries around the world, a more niche,
market-driven way of shopping still existed. I had always particularly
admired the custom of going to a bakery to get bread or to the cheese-
monger to get cheese. The idea that there were specialists you sought
out for each ingredient felt noteworthy. The concept of food being intentional and meaningful—as opposed to an afterthought—appealed
to me. I wanted cupcakes to feel like a worthwhile destination, not just
convenience.

So I set to work on becoming a cupcake specialist, developing the
best cupcake anyone had ever tasted—in twenty different flavors.
Charles and I blind taste-tested dozens of variations and made notes as
if we were expert sommeliers. I would number the different variations on
vanilla, chocolate, or strawberry and place them on plates that filled our
dining room table, each one marked by a hand-scribbled note announc-
ing its number in the lineup. Then we tasted and wrote down our observations, cleansing our palates with water as we went.

Just when I thought I had perfected the Sprinkles menu, Charles
pointed out that red velvet was missing from the lineup of flavors. To be
clear, it wasn't an oversight on my part. If I'm being totally honest, I had
never liked red velvet cake. In fact, I found it kind of tasteless. Most red
velvet cake recipes were essentially a flavorless cake, with the occa-
sional tablespoon of cocoa—mostly distinguished by the bright red hue
taken from food coloring. Charles insisted that I reconsider my decision.
Back in his home state, red velvet cake was as prevalent as vanilla or
chocolate might be, and I would not be doing his Oklahoma roots justice

without a red velvet on the menu. I capitulated but was steadfast in my quest to improve on the red velvets I had eaten in my past, bumping up the cocoa quotient to produce a more elegant chocolate profile, toning down the food coloring, and then bringing it all home with a rich and tangy cream cheese frosting. When we first opened our doors in Los Angeles, there were plenty of people who had never heard of red velvet cake before. I fielded confused requests for "that red cherry cupcake" or "the red carpet cupcake." But everyone quickly caught on and the resulting flavor became our bestselling cupcake. Thanks, Charles!

THINK OUTSIDE THE (CAKE) BOX

Imagine looking at the world and seeing opportunities where others don't. This type of vision is what helps entrepreneurs spot a gap in the market or imagine a business where no one else has. It's critical for finding a niche and then building a product or service to fill a need. Developing a unique insight that comes from your experience is key, but then thinking with an outsider's perspective allows you to pinpoint truly out-of-the-box business ideas.

My family and friends were generally pretty supportive while we built our business plan. But, once it was clear that Sprinkles was going to swim instead of sink, they felt free to let us know how worried they had been when the end result wasn't so clear. An old friend later revealed that after I confided in her about my plans to open Sprinkles, she fretted to her husband about me betting my life savings on something as frivolous as cupcakes. Charles's parents were also concerned. Their son, who'd spent a couple of years and a sizable amount of money on an MBA, wasn't using it to his advantage to climb a corporate ladder, and they were worried about him being able to support his family. And frankly, everyone was concerned about the timing of it all.

To be fair, I was opening a temple to carbs at the *height* of the low-carb craze. Not only that, but I was also opening it in Los Angeles—a city known for its obsession with health, wellness, and achieving the perfect physique. But as Charles and I drove around Los Angeles, we noticed something other Angelenos conveniently overlooked: multiple strip centers featuring myriad burger joints and donut shops. We suspected there was an appetite for more than just green juice in this town—and, it turns out, we were right. How could we see it when others couldn't? Well, we were literal outsiders, and that perspective served us well.

It's hard to go against the pack. We're social animals, and most of us don't want to be the lone wolf. But the irony is that once you venture forth and find success doing something differently, you become everyone's hero. Eventually, initial interest leads to widespread adoption, and pretty soon you've integrated right back into the pack again.

Call it rebellious, not buying into groupthink, having a different perspective, or whatever you want, I believe the best entrepreneurs possess a way of seeing things that others don't. Lean into this irreverent perspective to start viewing things in new ways. It will lead to creativity and innovation and keep you ahead of the curve. Outsider thinkers have the ability to revolutionize industries by breaking the established rules. Remember, the moment before something's a breakthrough, it's a crazy idea.

HOW TO SPOT OPPORTUNITY

Entrepreneurs see something others don't. They look where no one else is looking and find openings where others bump against walls. Here are three ways to help you find your unique idea.

Ask (a Lot of) Questions

This may go without saying, but I'll say it anyway. To spot an opportunity, you have to be actively looking for it. Question everything. Do not take things at face value. Your ears should perk up whenever you hear "Oh, that's just the way it's done," "That's the industry standard," or "That will never work!"

Enjoy Learning

Expertise helps! Being immersed within an industry, or having a good deal of knowledge about it, makes spotting opportunities easier. Even if you have no experience or education on a subject matter, you can become an expert on anything you find interesting enough to make time to pursue. You can also find a mentor in your desired industry to help kick-start your learning.

Steer Clear of Groupthink

As human beings we often conform our thinking to the larger group, but entrepreneurs must cultivate out-of-the-box thinking. The next time you're in a room of people that sounds like an echo chamber, run for the hills. Examine your own routine. Do you get your news from the same source every day? It's time to broaden your sources. If your habits are locked in, most likely your mindset is too.

FOOD FOR THOUGHT

Your expertise and unique perspective could be the key ingredients to spotting a successful opportunity that others don't see. Ask yourself these questions:

What personal experience or knowledge do you have that could yield an idea you are uniquely positioned to provide?

Do you feel passionately enough about your idea to move forward without much buy-in from others?

Are you comfortable challenging the status quo? What are some small ways you can practice doing so in your daily life?

Step Four

MAKE THE RECIPE YOUR OWN

*You don't have to reinvent the wheel,
but you should put your spin on it.*

arly in my career, when Sprinkles was just an idea in my head, I visited a friend at her lake house in Michigan. One of her favorite pastimes was shopping at the local vintage stores. This might be an unpopular opinion, but I have a bit of an aversion to vintage stores. Where most people see treasure, I see dust and clutter. I'm a minimalist at heart. And, if you've ever been inside a Sprinkles bakery, you would see that I'm drawn to modern, functional, and edited design. More than aesthetics, it probably also has something to do with the rather large collection of Asian antiques that my parents amassed during their years abroad. They were uncomfortable, unwieldy, and followed my family in crates on ships every time we moved. As a result, I like my stuff like I like my cupcakes: simple.

Still, I agreed to tag along and found myself taken in by the cookbook section. If anything could change my mind about an antique store, it would be vintage cookbooks; they are actually a lot of fun! I found it fascinating to see how food trends have evolved through the decades. Sandwiched between the *Woman's Day* back issues and the Jell-O mold cookbooks, one in particular caught my eye: *Martinis & Whipped Cream*.

As I thumbed through the yellowed pages, it dawned on me that this was a low-carb diet cookbook, espousing the very same principles as the "revolutionary" diet craze sweeping the country at the time: Atkins. My mind was blown to realize that the "New Diet Revolution" wasn't new or revolutionary after all, but rather a retread of the diet book I was look-ing at, published thirty years earlier!

Though Dr. Robert Atkins, the cardiologist behind the bestselling diet book in history at the time, had patented this dietary regime, it was clearly not an entirely new concept. *Martinis & Whipped Cream* served as an important reminder that breakthrough ideas don't have to be in-vented from scratch every time. They can also be *reinvented*.

Let's be clear: I am not implying that "nothing's new." In fact, quite the contrary. I have a massive appreciation for category inventors. Women swear by Spanx, which brought a whole new line of apparel. Or, what about Airbnb, Uber, and Netflix—all of which invented new categories that never existed—and as a result experienced faster growth and re-ceived higher valuations from investors than companies that bring incre-mental innovations to market.

But my goal is to encourage you to jump into entrepreneurship, and nothing could be more intimidating than saying you must create a new category. Especially when you really don't! What I have learned, and experienced myself, is that innovation doesn't mean dreaming up an entirely new idea. Effectively improving on something that already exists can be not only revolutionary but also an excellent business opportunity.

There are so many examples, like the recent rise of Peloton. Who would have thought that stationary cycling could be reinvented yet again? SoulCycle had already recently put a new spin on the spin cate-gory, but Peloton built upon the communal energy that SoulCycle started by offering a great at-home product, complete with virtual community. It shook the status quo but still resonated—igniting further during the pandemic when everyone was stuck at home and looking for ways to re-create group exercise.

We can't talk about reinventing the wheel without mentioning Bumble. The world of dating apps was already crowded when Whitney Wolfe founded Bumble. But her "Sadie Hawkins dance"–style twist of requiring women to make the first move was seen as an advancement for women and the digital dating category at large. The concept was certainly validated with millions of paying customers, and a $2 billion IPO that put Bumble alongside the longtime industry leader, Match Group.

A "new" idea doesn't have to be completely original to be groundbreaking. A simple twist, or different perspective on an existing, successful idea, can absolutely deliver a whole new value proposition.

SOMETIMES IT'S ABOUT REPACKAGING

I'm a big believer that the best ideas are already right in front of us—they just need to be reframed. I know this firsthand. With Sprinkles, we didn't invent cupcakes. They've have been around since the late 1700s when Amelia Simmons described "a cake to be baked in small cups" in *American Cookery*, though most food historians give credit to Eliza Leslie as the "Mother of the Cupcake," as she was the first to use the word in print. Later, Hostess made its mark as the first to mass-produce a single-portioned "snack cake" in 1919 (the power of repackaging) and, in 1950, it advanced cupcakes further by filling them with cream.

My innovation was to elevate the cupcake from a mass-produced kids' confection into an artisanal creation. I reinvented a supermarket treat by trading commonplace elements for top-shelf ingredients, and a childish aesthetic for one that was all grown up. The result was an elevated item that scaled beyond lunchbox fare and into something that would be a treasured gift. I offered this new breed to the world in a "cupcake only" bakery—the first of its kind. Remarkably, it had never been done, which certainly gave me pause, but I knew there was an opportunity to recast something everyone already loved.

IMPROVE IT BY REMOVING IT

We know founders can successfully innovate by taking a popular product and doubling down on what's working. But, what about improving a product by taking out aspects that *don't* work? This is how Native Deodorant approached their new deodorant, when they removed the aluminum, parabens, and sulfates present in legacy brands like Secret, Dove, and Degree. It turned out to be such a good idea that Native reached $100 million in revenue in two years and sold to Procter & Gamble because founder Moiz Ali said he couldn't keep up with the rapid growth.

This was also the idea behind organic supermarket favorite Annie's—whose mac and cheese is my sons' lunch of choice. In 1984, when Annie Withey was twenty-one, she and her then-husband, Andrew Martin, created a Cheddar popcorn in their kitchen. It was an all-natural cheese popcorn recipe that used white (not neon orange) cheddar cheese. They called it Smartfood. (Yes, that delicious healthy-ish popcorn you can now buy anywhere.)

It became quite a hit on its own and would eventually grow into the Annie's brand. Withey liked to use the Smartfood cheese mixture to make mac and cheese, again swapping out the conventional artificial orange for something more natural. After they sold Smartfood to Frito-Lay in 1989 for $15 million, Annie started making mac and cheese for the masses, first selling it out of her car trunk. Founded with the mission of upholding "sustainable agriculture, organic ingredients, no artificial ingredients [and] support for farmers and communities," Annie's went public in 2012, was purchased by General Mills in 2014 for $820 million, and is now the second-most popular mac and cheese brand in the United States behind Kraft. By taking something out, Annie's was able to add something new, and now highly coveted, to the previously similarly stocked supermarket shelves.

IMPORT IT!

You can also find founts of ideas overseas. Why not repackage something that is already working in another market? One of the greatest examples of this is Starbucks. On a trip to Italy in the early 1980s, Howard Schultz became enchanted by the ritual of Italians congregating around coffee bars sipping their espressos. He ultimately fell in love with the *caffè* culture of Italy and wanted to bring that magic back home. As he describes how he felt in his book *Pour Your Heart into It:* "I felt the unexpressed demand for romance and community. The Italians had turned the drinking of coffee into a symphony, and it felt right." Clearly Schultz did a brilliant job of adapting the Italian coffee culture experience to American tastes: adding seating, increasing portion sizes, offering convenient locations and to-go cups.

Keep in mind the complexities when translating a product to another culture. You want to be able to bring the product to your market respectfully, while avoiding cultural exploitation or appropriation. There's also the challenge of educating the consumer about a new product or, at least, a new way of looking at something they already know they like a certain way.

Case in point: Charles and I discovered Liège waffles while on our honeymoon. We fell in love with these warm, caramelized handheld snacks sold out of waffle carts. We obsessed over the idea of bringing them back to the States. However, as taken as we were with the product, we knew that the education involved in bringing back this cultural delicacy would be significant, given that Americans associate waffles with a plated breakfast. Starting a business is difficult enough, without the added layer of having to do unnecessarily heavy lifting around product education.

Since then, I've seen ambitious entrepreneurs compelled to import this tasty treat, including the Press Waffle Company, which made an appearance on *Shark Tank*, and another offering called Vafels, based in Boulder, Colorado, which added its own spin by using plant-based and organic ingredients. Only time will tell if the Belgian tradition takes off in a major way stateside, but it's exciting to see the original inspiration evolve in new ways.

FIX SOMETHING THAT'S DRIVING YOU CRAZY

Entrepreneurs and personal development gurus widely promote the value of optimism and positive thinking. They assert that optimism is good for your mental health and that it helps achieve lofty goals. I agree. Optimism was central to my opening the first-ever cupcakes-only bakery at the height of the low-carb craze.

But, while I believe in the benefit of positivity, I also maintain that there are upsides to keeping an eye out for seeing the negative—and leaning into it. Sometimes frustration is the greatest source of inspiration.

For example, Siete Family Foods founder Veronica Garza was suffering from autoimmune conditions that left her fatigued, overweight, and depressed when her brother suggested a low-inflammation, grain-free diet. In a show of moral support, her family joined in switching out the ingredients making her sick. But, as Mexican Americans from South Texas, they found that the tacos and fajitas that they loved on flour and corn tortillas just weren't as satisfying on a lettuce leaf. Looking for a fix to her frustration, Garza began making grain-free tortillas with almond flour. She knew she was onto something when her grandmother said her tortillas tasted better than the homemade flour ones she'd made for decades. With Abuela's vote of confidence, the family started selling their grain-free products to local grocery stores. Today, Siete Family Foods, named for this family of seven, is available nationwide across thousands of supermarkets. And, the brand is enabling healthier eating in a category that, until the Garza family came in, had not seen cassava, chickpea, or cashew flours—or this kind of innovation.

So the next time you try to stop yourself from being "negative" and force yourself to look on the bright side, stop. Lean into what is frustrating *you*. You'll probably end up solving a problem and perhaps even coming up with your next great idea.

TURN A TREND INTO A CATEGORY DISRUPTER

When Gail Becker decided to start a business making gluten-free cauliflower pizza crusts, she had no food experience. What she lacked in culinary expertise, Gail more than made up for in business acumen. Having overseen her fair share of multimillion-dollar businesses, she knew how to run a company. But, also having spent years successfully climbing the corporate ladder, she found herself disenchanted once she'd surveyed her view from the top as a senior executive. "When you stop caring about your work, it's a good warning sign," she says.

When Gail's father passed away, it sparked a deep desire to put her energy toward something with which she felt a real connection. She didn't have to search long or hard to be inspired. As the mother of two sons with celiac disease, Gail already spent a lot of time in the kitchen creating gluten-free alternatives for her boys from scratch. One such recipe was a cauliflower pizza crust. Well, there wasn't just one recipe; there were more than half a million floating around online. Cauliflower crust was definitely trending. The only problem? It took ninety minutes to make.

"Ninety minutes is too long to make a pizza crust," Gail decided. So, in 2016, she left her high-powered corporate job to follow a gut feeling that people would want a convenient, healthier alternative to frozen pizza. In February 2017, CAULIPOWER launched in thirty-seven Whole Foods locations and has since grown to be on the shelves of thirty thousand stores.

When CAULIPOWER hit the freezer section, there was nothing like it in the frozen pizza category, but like any successful product, it has inspired a slew of imitators. Since launch, there have been about fifty new SKUs from about twenty different brands. It's grown into one of the most competitive categories in the grocery store. CAULIPOWER was up against some pretty big names like Kraft and Green Giant, but with a great-tasting product, a strong brand, and loyal customers, it continues to reign as the top cauliflower pizza crust.

How did CAULIPOWER find success?

- **First to market.** CAULIPOWER moved fast and disrupted an entire category that prevented competitors from breaking through.
- **Strong brand.** CAULIPOWER has done a good job of standing out in a crowded shelf with a strong, recognizable brand voice that invokes irreverence and joy.

- **Education to a broader market.** Though it was the genesis for its inception, CAULIPOWER does not lead with gluten-free messaging. The gluten-free crowd is only a small segment of their customers; many people just wanted a healthier alternative, so the product needed to be positioned as such. But even the gluten-free audience needed education because they didn't know a gluten-free product could actually taste good.

- **Superior product.** Compared to competitors, CAULIPOWER has always tasted the best. When it comes to a food product, the winning trifecta is taste, health, and convenience. It's easy to achieve one, hard to get two, and almost impossible to get three. CAULIPOWER is a triple threat.

- **Anticipate demand.** It was hard to keep up with a growing demand, but Gail was savvy enough to know that competitors would closely follow, so she prioritized distribution to stay ahead of the pack.

FOOD FOR THOUGHT

Often, the most successful business ideas aren't completely original. If you're looking for your next big idea, consider these questions:

What are some pain points you've experienced in your day-to-day?

Do you love something but have always had an idea for how to make it better?

Is there a popular product you love that's due for a refresh?

Step Five

TEST THE APPETITE

Is the world hungry for your idea?

C an one phone call really change everything? It did for me. And never in a million years would I have expected it to be from a producer for *The Tyra Banks Show.*

In 2003, with the dream of opening a risky new venture, Charles and I left San Francisco—where the economy was still suffering from the dot-com bust—for Los Angeles, where the economy was more diversified and still thriving. I began toiling away in our West Hollywood apartment kitchen, baking a new kind of gourmet cupcake. As word got out, orders poured in—first from friends, and then friends of friends, and then complete strangers. Word spread to the point where I stopped being able to trace the source.

Such was the case with Tyra's TV show producer, who had developed a fondness for my cupcakes and called to order a batch as a gift for Tyra's thirtieth birthday.

Somehow, I had nabbed my first celebrity client—while working from my tiny rental apartment. At the time, I didn't realize that I was building validation for my product. Silicon Valley investors call it "product-market fit," and it's when customers are clamoring for your product. Product-market fit is the holy grail of technology start-ups, with new companies iterating on their product until they can prove signs of having achieved it. And once they do, funding comes easily. Perhaps because I'm a baker, though, I like to think of product-market fit more as an appetite.

I initially tested that appetite by selling directly from my apartment. I started baking for my friends, then their friends would taste the cupcakes and call to place their order, and so on. It was a financially prudent way for me to evaluate the market before going all-in on a retail space, and it allowed me to collect customer feedback in a low-stakes setting. With this minimal overhead and investment, I was able to discover that I had some traction, an early sign that my idea had "legs."

HOT TIP

An early marker of product-market fit is an organic, exponential demand for your product. Because, whether or not your product is a cupcake, you need to make sure people are hungry for it.

But relying on my small network of friends in a new city would not be enough to spread the Sprinkles gospel. So I did whatever it took to get my product in customers' hands. I drove all over town, delivering hand-crafted cupcakes for baby showers and birthday parties. I set up cupcake "stations" at local trunk shows and craft fairs. I gave away samples, ordered business cards, and eagerly tried to get both into people's hands. In today's lingo, I was "product seeding," but at that point I had never even heard the term!

In 2005, there weren't any platforms like Instagram or Facebook to instantly introduce a brand to the exact right demographic and wait for the flood of customers. You had to go to the customers—literally. I brought cupcakes to hotel concierges as well as local fire and police departments and donated them to charitable events. I even took them to the top salons (more on that later). My efforts ultimately started a buzz that led to my first high-profile client—Tyra Banks—and subsequently getting a feature on her show.

HOT TIP

Keep your ego in check. You never know what will lead to the big opportunity! Just like a politician running for office, sometimes you'll show up to screaming crowds and sometimes you can hear the sound of crickets. But you have to keep showing up and kissing babies!

PINPOINT A PROBLEM

Based on customer feedback and increasing demand, I suspected we were onto a good idea. But I wasn't sure there was an actual problem that we were solving. And isn't that fundamentally what a business is supposed to do? Albert Einstein is often quoted as having said, "If I were given one hour to save the planet, I would spend fifty-nine minutes defining the problem and one minute resolving it." I knew I needed to ask more questions to get to the root of the problem I was trying to solve. So, I dug deep into my own past experiences.

I fondly remembered the days of office culture, when ordering a cake for someone's birthday was always a hassle. There was the search for mismatched plates, knives, and forks from takeout lunches past. Don't forget the "not me" game of cleanup. And, inevitably, someone hated chocolate or carrot cake with raisins and needed everyone to know that they couldn't partake. Cupcakes were the perfect solution. No fork or knife necessary—even a plate was optional. Most importantly, with an individual treat, everyone got to pick the one that suited their palate.

In the office and beyond, cakes had been the default for birthdays and special celebrations because they looked and tasted special. If cupcakes looked and tasted like kids' food, they never stood a chance. But, if they could truly stack up against occasion cakes, I believed they would become the natural choice for celebrations of every kind.

Baked goods have historically been an accessible and thoughtful handmade gift. But busy modern life rarely allows time to create a home-baked treat if one even has the inclination. By elevating cupcakes, I was also solving for an easily purchased gift with the hallmarks of being heartfelt and homemade. And, because the Sprinkles brand stood for quality, these cupcakes could also stand up against traditional luxury gifts like designer candles, chocolates, or flowers.

IS IT A BIG-ENOUGH PROBLEM?

If you had asked most people if there was a need for an upscale cupcake or a cupcake-only bakery, most would have emphatically said no. But as Steve Jobs said about Apple's strategy for solving a need: "Some people say give the customers what they want, but that's not my approach. Our job is to figure out what they're going to want before they do."

Of course, we all know this to be true (especially if you're currently reading this on your iPhone or iPad). Earlier I mentioned how important it was to make sure there is a "hunger" for your product. The truth is, sometimes people don't even know if and when they're hungry. Take your TikTok feed, for example. You'll be scrolling, feeling perfectly fine, when—*bam!*—you see the latest viral food sensation. Suddenly, you're salivating. Sometimes it's necessary to present the problem that you're fixing for people to even realize they have a problem.

It's also critical to provide a strong-enough solution to that problem that someone would be willing to pay (potentially even at a premium) for it? If so, how many people? One way to try to answer that question is to research the size of your potential market.

When we launched Sprinkles, there wasn't an artisanal cupcake market in existence—we created it. But this didn't let us off the hook for doing our homework. We still had a great big market for celebratory desserts. When you consider the fact that everyone has a birthday once a year, the market was fairly sizable, and our big opportunity.

When the founders of Airbnb were pitching their idea to investors, they had to prove that the controversial idea of "sharing your home with a stranger" was a viable market ready to be tapped. This is why its original pitch deck included two key data points: "630,000 listings on couchsurfing.com" and "17,000 temporary housing listings on SF & NYC Craigslist." They also shared the experience of the first time they advertised their "air bed and breakfast" (spend the night on an air mattress on their living room floor for $80), when five hundred people responded. What's truly amazing is how their idea went from crashing on air mattresses to emerging as an actual threat to the hospitality industry. Today it's essentially the largest hotel chain in the world—taking up more market share than the world's top five hotel chains put together. In advance of its initial public offering, Airbnb listed its "total addressable market" as $3.4 trillion.

DETERMINE YOUR MARKET SIZE

Unlike Airbnb, I was not pitching venture capitalists (VCs) on my idea. Knowing what I know now, it would never have received funding. My idea sounded so gratuitous that I couldn't even get potential landlords to call me back. So I bootstrapped it.

Even though the market wasn't the right size for investors, it turned out to be the right size for me. Because I had enough money saved from my previous jobs to bankroll my initial launch, I didn't need to find a billion-dollar market or promise fiftyfold returns to get the first store up and running—both of which VCs would want to see before they agreed to invest. As long as I could maintain a cash flow and continue to scale the business, the only buy-in I needed was from new customers.

Ultimately, it depends on what your business goals are. If you want to start a small, local business to make a comfortable living, that's one thing.

But if you are building a company you plan to scale that will require outside funding, you'd better have a good handle on your market size because it's one of the most important things that professional investors consider. Venture capital investors are looking to invest in concepts that address large markets that could potentially scale globally. Simply put, they are looking for a financial return that is in line with the extra risk they are taking by investing in an early-stage company. Even if you create a valuable solution to a thorny problem, if the market isn't large enough or growing quickly with plenty of opportunity, investors will take their dollars elsewhere. Remember, it's not just about providing an innovative, sellable solution, it's also demonstrating that lots and lots of people want it.

STRESS-TEST YOUR IDEA

Addressing the market is only one part of the process. Back when I launched Sprinkles, I could have beat my drum all day long about the multibillion-dollar market for desserts, but if no one had found my cupcakes delicious, it wouldn't have mattered one bit. So, I first tested—and proved—demand for my product by selling my cupcakes on a smaller scale.

Stress-testing your idea is a sound strategy and it can take many different forms. Here are some approaches to consider:

- Put up a landing page to build a waitlist or presell your product
- Research the monthly search term volume related to your product
- Use surveys or conduct interviews with potential customers
- Seed the product to a test group and gather feedback
- Consign your product in stores or sell through Etsy
- Build a working prototype or create a mockup with a 3D printer
- Presell your new product on a crowdfunding platform like Kickstarter

You don't even need to have the whole product worked out before going to market. The term *minimum viable product* (*MVP*) is used to describe the most basic, stripped-back model of a product that can be used to test customer demand and then learn what needs to be added or changed before launch. Testing your assumptions before you've invested in all the bells and whistles is a great idea. It allows flexibility to adjust your offering to better suit the needs of the market before going all-in.

Remember the story of Native Deodorant? Moiz Ali knew he wanted to create a natural deodorant but didn't know if people would buy it online, as it's usually thrown into a drugstore pickup. So, he launched Native on the website Product Hunt (a community-based website where you can launch and get feedback on new products) without an actual product. He received fifty presale orders. Only after he had this initial validation that there might be demand for his product did he place his first order—for one hundred units with a mom-and-pop manufacturer.

I can't emphasize enough that you don't have to build out an entire line when launching a new product. Test the market and gain traction with an initial "hero product" before expanding on your idea. This is exactly what Everlane did when they launched with cotton T-shirts in 2011, *before* moving into a whole line of clothing basics. Founder Michael Preysman says: "What a really great company does is figure out, 'What are the customer's needs?' And then [give] it to them." Since then, Everlane has added other product groups—sweaters, jackets, and accessories—all while retaining its original promise of radical transparency, ethical production, and a focus on sustainability.

PLAY WHERE NO ONE IS LOOKING

I'll never forget a chart that Charles and I saw in *Entrepreneur* magazine, which laid out a variety of industries and the prospective payoff for each. Tech and finance—where we had just come from—was on the far right, the big-money category. Bakery and retail—where we were now pouring all our energies—was on the far left, with much less money to be made and a much lower chance of success!

We marveled about us leaving those lucrative categories to opt for the industry with the dreary outlook. What were we thinking? But sometimes this type of picture doesn't show the whole story.

When there's seemingly no opportunity, fewer people are sniffing around. That means there's less competition and less innovation. These forgotten industries can be great markets. That's what the bakery industry was: generational family-owned businesses that had not been disrupted in decades. No one saw it as a place for opportunity, which is why it was actually perfect.

Going for sleepy markets can be a great strategy. Everyone is chasing new technologies, but things that have been around for long periods of time—legacy industries—get ignored. No one was thinking about razors when Michael Dubin started Dollar Shave Club. There was no innovation in how they would be sold—they were going to be stuck on a shelf at Walgreens forever. Alexandra Friedman wasn't looking at newcomers when she entered the feminine care category with LOLA. And hair color was pretty dull when Amy Errett disrupted the space with Madison Reed. While the market wasn't vibrant, it was big—in 2020 the global hair color market was $23.2 billion. Each of these founders had to face giant consumer packaged goods (CPG) competitors with established brands and huge advertising budgets, but their innovation helped them stand out, and there was room and reason for consumers to pay attention.

FOOD FOR THOUGHT

Before you go all-in with your passion, it's wise to test the market before making any big moves. Once you have an idea, ask yourself these questions:

Does your product or idea solve a real problem?

How big a problem is it? How many people could potentially benefit from your solution?

In what way can you test demand for your product on a small scale?

Step Six

STIR IN RESOLVE

Cultivate resilience in the midst of setbacks.

Growing up, I worshiped the advertising execs on *Melrose Place*—especially Amanda Woodward, an iconic performance by Heather Locklear. I was glued to the screen as she strutted around her glossy advertising office, delegating commands in sharp suits and towering heels. She was the epitome of power, and even then I wanted to know what that felt like.

Interestingly, the past decade has turned the spotlight from salaried executives like Amanda Woodward to entrepreneurs like Walter White. (Okay, maybe not *just* like Walter White.) We see them exalted on TV, grace the covers of glossy magazines, and become the subject of feature films—even tabloid fodder. While the ad execs of yesteryear were glamorous and powerful (hello, Don Draper), entrepreneurs, though much more stereotypically casually dressed, are even more romanticized.

Liberated from the shackles of corporate America, they follow their passions and make millions from nothing. Entrepreneurs are unstoppable! Right? Well . . . yes and no.

I won't lie, overseeing your destiny and creating something out of very little is an indescribable high—but there's a much less exciting side as well. To put it plainly, it's not easy, and I'm one of the lucky ones. I'm fortunate enough to be surrounded by many other female founders. We see each other at panels, dinners, and events, understanding each other with knowing smiles, nods, and furtive looks across the room like we've taken a tacit oath of sisterhood. When we talk, we ask how it's going—and then we drop all pretense to ask how it's *really* going. To the rest of the world, it looks effortless, but if you're in the club, you know it's not as easy-breezy as social media feeds demand we make it look.

KEEP CALM AND CARRY ON

It may seem as though I really lucked out on my first foray into entrepreneurship, but there was a failed business idea that preceded Sprinkles. After graduating pastry school, I had my first entrepreneurial epiphany—I should open my own cooking school. The concept was loosely based on the school I attended in San Francisco, Tante Marie's, which offered both professional and nonprofessional classes, as well as corporate team-building events. I began looking at real estate in Dallas, where we were considering relocating. The city didn't have a great cooking school, and I believed it was ready for one. I even found an amazing retail space in a great location. It was going to be perfect. All the chips were falling into place for my new entrepreneurship dream to come alive. My whole future unfolded in front of my eyes—until the next time we visited the building. We pulled up to check it out, only to find a new sign out front: "Coming soon: Viking Cooking School." A *cooking school?* I mean, what were the chances?

I was consumed with disappointment. I had poured so much creative energy into planning a future that centered around a cooking school. So, when the lights went out on my idea, I was despondent. I was going to have to start *again*? From scratch? It seemed so daunting to have to basically call a do-over. In life, I'm a firm believer that things happen for a reason. Though it was hard for me to accept the reality at the time, Viking Cooking School had done me a big fat favor. My heartache would prove to be the fuel I needed to become a better entrepreneur. It was a lesson in resilience, patience, and trusting that there was something better waiting for me.

For me to find my next great idea, I would have to abandon the old one, no matter how attached I had become. Most important, I would have to do it quickly. There is an opportunity cost to spending time on anything that doesn't bring you closer to realizing your goals. When you've tested the appetite and found it lacking because of the market, competition, or timing, cut your losses and pivot to something more promising.

HANDLE THE HEAT

Not everyone is falling in love with your product? You have company. Rejection is one theme central to every entrepreneur's story. But it's how you handle the heat and commit to staying in the kitchen or repositioning yourself for something better that will determine your success.

VIEW SETBACKS AS OPPORTUNITIES

I landed in Los Angeles, "the City of Dreams," in 2003, motivated and hopeful about my new cupcake bakery idea, the setback in Dallas now firmly in my rearview mirror. But reality quickly set in. It was the height of a booming economy, which meant a tight real estate market. In other words, rents were high, available locations were scarce, and good spaces were impossible to find. Charles and I hopped in the same trusty car that had delivered those cakes over the impossible hills of San Francisco and drove all over LA County—from beachside Venice all the way to inland Pasadena—in our quest for the perfect spot for our cupcake bakery. I called the numbers on every "For Lease" sign to inquire about spaces that fit my parameters. I left dozens and dozens of messages, and not a single landlord called me back. When I was able to get a live human on the other end of the phone, they were reliably unimpressed with my idea. "What else will you sell?" was the constant refrain. Some even hung up before I had a chance to answer.

It was the classic chicken-and-egg scenario. How was I going to get a break with no track record? In a hot real estate market, no one wanted to take a chance on such a risky venture with a novice entrepreneur attached.

There were no less than three mediocre locations that I seriously considered out of sheer desperation. I went far down these roads too, negotiating leases and bringing on an architect to draw up plans for the space. Yet for various reasons, each of those locations fell through.

It seemed like my dream would never happen. I remember breaking down one day out of total frustration. Should I give up? When you hear "no" enough times, it starts to really wear on your resolve. While I was melting down (I'm the passionate one, clearly), Charles remained steadfast, believing the right location would come along. See, the cost of a bad location is almost always higher than waiting to find the right one. There's no liquidity once you build it out, sign a lease, and educate customers on where to find you. So, you'd better be sure it's the right spot.

I was trying to remain calm, trying to see this as a sign, like the Viking Cooking School. There comes a point in every venture when you must weigh risk versus regret. My litmus test was to ask myself a simple question: *If I don't do this, will I always regret it?* For me, the regret I knew I would feel by not pursuing this idea outweighed any risk I was taking. I could not throw in the towel, no matter how frustrated I felt.

Ultimately, we landed on a tiny sandwich spot on a sleepy street in Beverly Hills and, as you might expect from a 90210 zip code, it was far from a good deal. We had to pay $100,000 for the "right" to take over the lease (this is called "key" money). The subsequent renovation took much longer and was much more costly than I ever imagined. But the risk proved to be worth it. And, to this day, whenever I drive past one of the other could-have-been locations, I breathe a sigh of gratitude for the different versions of Sprinkles that never were. I believe that the Sprinkles of Venice or mid-city LA would have experienced a very different trajectory.

CAN YOU ANSWER THIS ONE SIMPLE QUESTION?

Is there anything else you can do?

This was the question posed to me by my theater professor in college. I was minoring in theater and had big dreams of pursuing an acting career after graduation. (I told you I was confused!) During a conversation with my professor, he challenged me with this statement: "If there's anything else you can do besides becoming an actor, do it."

At the time, I was completely caught off guard by his brash honesty. Wasn't his role to encourage me? My early adult confidence faltered and, ultimately, I buckled. I knew there were plenty of other career avenues I could pursue, so I did.

I now realize that my professor was challenging my resolve. He knew how difficult it is to choose the life of a working actor, and he wanted to spare me from that pain if I wasn't 100 percent committed. He was asking me, in effect, if there was a plan B. And at the time, there was, so I took it.

Today, I pose the same question to you: Is there anything else you can do besides becoming an entrepreneur? If you can pass on your business idea and sleep at night, then it's probably not for you. The life of an entrepreneur is one of equal parts ecstasy and tragedy. Sounds dramatic? It is. Hey, maybe I didn't really choose a plan B after all.

RISE AGAIN

Who remembers the early 2000s sock puppet from Pets.com? Behind that puppet is a real person. Her name is Julie Wainwright, and she was the CEO of Pets.com—which promptly went out of business exactly 268 days after its IPO—making it "one of the shortest-lived public companies on record," according to Kirk Cheyfitz, author of *Thinking Inside the Box: The 12 Timeless Rules for Managing a Successful Business.*

The real icing on this burnt cake? On the very same day she was forced to lay off two hundred employees, her husband asked for a divorce. "It was just like a dark cloud descended," Wainwright says.

Eventually that cloud parted, and in true entrepreneurial fashion, she was struck with a new business idea. Like my experience finding inspiration while browsing vintage cookbooks, Julie's stroke of genius struck while shopping with a friend for secondhand items. Her friend said that she didn't trust consignment shops or eBay because it was too easy to pass off knockoffs as the real deal. Buying secondhand luxury items from a shopkeeper she knew and trusted was the only way she felt comfortable making these types of purchases.

Wainwright saw an opportunity—an online store for authenticated preowned luxury goods. There was a big market: some $50 billion a year for personal luxury items. But it wasn't easy for her to make a comeback. Challenges included being a woman in her mid-fifties pitching male VCs and being known as the leadership responsible for the Pets.com flop.

"Even though the tech industry says they don't mind losers, it's not true; they hate losers," she says. "I definitely wallowed in it too long, and at some point, I had [to] give myself a pep talk. I got back to what was important to me." She found resilience and founded The RealReal, which has raised hundreds of millions in venture capital. In 2019, the company went public—and this time it stayed that way. Just like punching down bread to watch it rise again, she discovered that the pounding she took for her first venture was necessary to stretch and shape her next creation. "You might just find that you have more," says Wainwright in a piece she wrote for *Forbes.* "More inner strength, more tenacity, more grit, more courage, more kindness, more compassion than you ever thought was possible."

I can relate to Julie's journey. I've learned to accept the fact that even when you plan for everything, anything could happen. The key is staying strong and committed yet open and nimble to new opportunities and connections.

FOOD FOR THOUGHT

Starting a business requires a thick skin, because you're likely to get a few burns. Before you decide to enter the world of entrepreneurship, ask yourself some tough questions:

How determined are you to make your idea work? What sacrifices will you have to make?

Can you pick yourself up from your failures, take the lessons, and move on? Do you have someone you can lean on to help deal with disappointment?

Would you feel incomplete if you do not pursue this business idea? Can you harness this feeling as motivation to propel you?

Step Seven

GET COOKING!

Now is the time to take action.

Ideas are a dime a dozen. Succeeding is all about action and execution. Many dream about starting their own company, but very few take the initiative—for good reason: It's a lot of hard work and a few strokes of luck.

When I first opened Sprinkles, several customers walked in and exclaimed, "This was *my* idea." They weren't insinuating I stole their vision, but rather that they, too, had dreamed of opening a cupcake bakery. The difference was that I had brought that dream into reality, and now they were literally standing in it. Believe it or not, an idea—even a great idea—is rarely novel.

• • • • •

IF YOU DON'T ACT,
YOUR IDEA MIGHT MOVE ON WITHOUT YOU.

In Elizabeth Gilbert's *New York Times* bestseller, *Big Magic: Creative Living beyond Fear*, she purports that our planet is inhabited not only by animals and plants and bacteria and viruses, but also by ideas, which are driven by a single impulse: to be made manifest. And the only way an idea can come to life is through human efforts to escort it out of the ether and into the realm of the material. Therefore, ideas spend eternity swirling around us searching for available and willing human partners. When an idea thinks it has found somebody who might be able to bring it into the world, the idea will try to get your attention. This is the Big Magic.

Some years ago, Big Magic visited an already successful Elizabeth Gilbert, and then just as easily vanished. She tells the uncanny story of being visited by a big idea: that she should write a novel about Brazil in the 1960s. Specifically, she felt inspired to write a novel about the real-life efforts to build an ill-fated highway across the jungle. Gilbert proceeded to do her research and write the story, until a real-life drama pulled her away from the novel. When she was finally able to return to her book years later, she found that the magic had escaped. She knew what had happened because she'd seen it before. The idea had grown tired of waiting and had left her. If inspiration is allowed to unexpectedly enter you, it is also allowed to unexpectedly exit you if left unattended.

Just around the same time the idea for her novel ran away in 2008, she happened to meet a fellow author, Ann Patchett, at a panel event. The two new friends began writing each other long, thoughtful letters every month. In autumn of that year, Ann casually mentioned in a letter that she had recently begun working on a new novel, and that it was about the Brazilian jungle, and for obvious reasons, it caught Elizabeth's attention. She mentioned she had a similar idea, but the idea went away because she neglected it.

When they met up a few months later, Elizabeth explained her book plot to Ann, who in turn told Elizabeth that her novel was almost identical. After the revelation, they retraced their steps to the day when

Elizabeth lost the idea, and Ann subsequently found it. It turns out those events occurred at the same time. In fact, it might have been officially transmitted on the day they met.

● ● ● ● ●

It's likely that you've never started a company before, but certainly you've set other goals throughout your life. Do you tend to meet them? Do you trust that when you make these goals, you will deliver? These smaller decisions in other areas of your life might not seem as though they mean much, but, ultimately, they are necessary building blocks to the self-reliance needed to forge your own path.

Oftentimes, I find that people get stuck on the *how*. If you're prone to perfectionism, it can be paralyzing because you never feel "ready." But, if there is anything I learned while earning what I like to call my "cupcake MBA," it's that you can, and oftentimes must, start the journey before you've plotted the map.

I know this may not be easy. It's certainly not how I've become wired, which is why I chose wisely in a business partner. My husband, Charles, has always been my counterbalance in this regard. While Charles never did his homework and went to the head of the class by confidently winging it, I was sitting front row, taking notes ad nauseam for fear that I would be called on and not know the answer (there's that imposter syndrome again). But I've learned that you can't be ready for everything that comes your way. How could you predict the dot-com bust would leave you without a job or prospects? Or how would you ever imagine you'd be baking cupcakes for *The Oprah Winfrey Show*? These are the surprises that you deal with on the fly—and construct a strategy for as you go.

There comes a time when you just must go for it. When opportunity knocks, you heed the call. No one's story illustrates this better than that of my friend Annie Campbell, a preeminent event caterer in Los Angeles. Annie is beloved by celebrities for her elegant events brimming with towering "naked" cakes, luxurious grilled cheeses, and signature herbaceous cocktails. But her road to coveted event planner was not exactly, well, planned!

Annie loved throwing parties and was terrific at it. She knew she wanted to pursue a career in food but didn't know what that would look like. Her friend Amy persistently nudged her to figure it out, until one day she just threw Annie into the fire. When someone asked Amy for a recommendation to help with a dinner party, she gave Annie's number to the prospective client.

Annie had never catered an event and now there was a woman on the phone asking if she could do a dinner for sixty people the next night. "Are you available?"

"Yes," Annie replied, without much thought.

Most people would have started sweating at that point, but Annie got to work. She created a menu, hit the farmers' market, made trips to Whole Foods, and asked a friend if she could act as a server. Annie stayed up twenty-four hours, cried on her way to the job, and then set up, passed the hors d'oeuvres, displayed the buffet, cleaned up—and impressed her first client.

Annie was hired again (and again), and word quickly spread about her flawless events, effortless style, and top-tier team. Years later, her business is booming as she has her sights set on a cookbook and a brick-and-mortar location. Does she know exactly how to do that? Of course not, but I know she'll figure out how to get it done.

FOLLOW THE BREAD CRUMBS

It can be hard to get started. Taking on a big project and creating something from nothing feels overwhelming. However, I've found that breaking the end goal down into manageable bites is the only way to stay consistent. Once you get traction, the rest will unfold.

I was planning to plunk down my life savings on starting a bakery without having had any experience working in one. I had spent a little time as a teen employed at a few restaurants as a host and server, but my partner Charles's only restaurant experience to date had been simply eating in them. So trust me when I say that neither one of us had the first clue how to open or operate a retail bakery. What I did know, and leaned into, was how to find people with more expertise than me, and how to ask the right questions.

While still working out of my apartment, I decided I needed a wholesale specialty food supplier—someone who could sell me my most expensive ingredients, such as Belgian chocolate and vanilla extract, at a discounted bulk price. Keep in mind, wholesale food suppliers supply restaurants, cafes, or bakeries, not bakers working out of their apartment. Of course, as far as I was concerned, it was only a matter of time before I would be one of those legitimate businesses, too, so I persuaded a salesperson over the phone to pay me a visit at my office—my home kitchen. I convinced him that, despite the very makeshift look of things, Sprinkles would become one of his biggest accounts one day. Spoiler: It did. He not only took a chance on me, but also became a very important source of education, teaching me about ingredient pricing and inventory management and guiding me on important health department protocols. Remember my advice about following the bread crumbs? Another very important bread crumb for me was a woman named Karen. She was the mom of a friend of a friend in Los Angeles who owned a small bakery on Pico Boulevard. I reached out to ask if I might come visit and ask her a few questions. Not only did she invite Charles and me to swing by at the end of her busy day at the bakery, but she also served us cookies and milk while teaching us which equipment to buy and how to schedule staff. She also kept her door open to us to stop by whenever we wanted, which we did. (Obviously, we couldn't turn down free advice, or her incredible chocolate chip cookies.) I'm so grateful for Karen's kindness and generosity. Now, not everyone has a mentor like that within their personal network, but there are amazing professional networks that can offer support. And we all have LinkedIn and social media, which means you could be just a few DMs away from your first important bread crumb.

Consider a mentor: If there is someone in your industry you could learn from, reach out to them and ask if they would consider mentoring you. People regularly ask me to become a mentor and I often oblige. A direct message on Instagram is exactly how I became a mentor to

Auzerais Bellamy, a professional pastry chef and founder of Blondery, a direct-to-consumer bakery. Auzerais followed me on social media, engaged with my content, and then reached out with a few questions. Our email exchange led to a phone call and the rest is history. Auzerais believes so strongly in the value of mentorship that she has assembled a *team* of mentors, five people, each with strength in a different area of business. She speaks to her mentors regularly on a variety of topics from legal and e-commerce to operations and strategy. Auzerais is careful to be respectful of her mentors' time and frequently sends blondies to "sweeten" the deal. That's what I call mastering mentorship!

> **You can choose to engage in your life and participate in it, or you can back out and criticize everybody else in your arena.**
>
> —*Gwyneth Paltrow, actress and founder of Goop*

THE DOER V. THE CRITIC

A t Sprinkles we were always amazed at the people who were quick to cut us down. We had worked hard to bring something special into the world. Why did people feel it necessary to be negative? This is when we were introduced to the idea of someone who is doing and acting in the world versus someone who is just commentating.

Which type of person do you want to be?

DOES THE RECIPE WORK?

Cupcakes quickly became a passion that fueled me into action. I relied on my gut (and taste buds) in the formation of the initial idea. But rest assured, I called upon my business experience to stress-test it. I knew if Charles and I were plunking down our life savings on what many said was a crazy scheme, we needed to back this thing up with some numbers. Although we had once been immersed in a world of financial models, company valuations, and IPO roadshow presentations, the official "business plan" for Sprinkles was incredibly basic. In fact, the original data used to support the concept was sketched on the back of a napkin on a road trip.

But, to know where to start, I had to answer some simple questions. No one had ever opened a cupcakes-only bakery before. And the first thing you must ask yourself is, *Why? Is there a good reason?* I built a rough model to understand the quantity we would need to sell every day to make it work and set out to answer several other questions:

- What exactly would be sold?
- How big was the market? (We discussed this in step 5.)
- Who would the customers be?
- How would it be marketed?
- Where would the store open?

Then I reverse-engineered the market. In other words, I thought about our expenses—rent, labor, insurance—and considered how many cupcakes, given an assumed profit margin, I would need to sell to cover those expenses. I came up with a number, considered the densely populated city of LA, and felt confident I could get to that number.

Answering a few basic questions and running some numbers was enough to give me comfort about the viability of my idea. "The business plan is overrated," Amar Bhide posits in his *Harvard Business Review* article, "Bootstrap Finance: The Art of Start-ups." "Traditional business-planning processes are less relevant to bootstrappers—where resilience trumps planning and energy trumps experience."

Instead of a fully hashed-out business plan, which can be intimidating, focus on the business model—how your company will make money. For my business, that answer was simple; I would make money selling cupcakes. However, for other businesses, particularly technology companies, it needs to be articulated. For example, does your app cost money to access or is it free and making money through advertising or affiliate deals? Even with businesses as straightforward as restaurants, the model isn't always as simple as "sell food." During the pandemic, most eateries had to entertain new business models, such as food subscription services, to survive. (I'll go into business models in depth in step 13.) Consider the various avenues for bringing in revenue, but don't overplan at this stage, because as an entrepreneur it will serve you to stay nimble.

FOOD FOR THOUGHT

Once you've decided your idea is ready for the green light, ask yourself the following questions before you step into full launch mode:

Are you ready to start taking action to make your dream a reality?

Have you identified the first few steps necessary to get started?

Do you have a mentor or industry insider who can help guide you?

Have you gathered the initial data to run some numbers or create a simple business plan?

Part Two

PACKAGE IT!

Embrace Your Inner Marketer

Ask anyone what they believe was the secret to Sprinkles' success and I guarantee you'll hear a mention of branding, design, and marketing. Yes, the product was amazing—you must have a product that people desperately want—but I would bet there are a lot of great products that will never see the level of recognition that my cupcakes saw. So what gives? I believe that the way Sprinkles was packaged and presented to the world is what made all the difference.

Now, most founders don't have any prior experience in marketing. Remember, I wasn't super credentialed in this department—I'd previously worked in finance and pastry. While anyone can be transformed into a founder by coming up with the right idea, you need to be a bit savvier to take on the other roles you can't yet afford to hire. In some ways, leading Sprinkles' marketing was a learning curve for me, and in other ways it was second nature because I was able to listen to my gut. Essentially, I designed a product I would love and marketed it in the way I would want to experience it as a customer.

The world of marketing has evolved by light-years since I first opened Sprinkles' doors in 2005. This was a pre-Instagram, pre-direct-to-consumer, pre-Facebook advertising void! But despite the many technological advances in our modern world, the one thing that hasn't changed much is the psychology behind a person's motivation and desire. Any good marketer is still laser-focused on the most basic premise of marketing: what drives people to purchase.

I remember first learning about marketing during a brief lesson on human psychology during my eighth-grade social studies class. Our teacher taught us that all advertising was meant to inspire a feeling, persuade, and ultimately, motivate behavior. I distinctly remember reading that every advertisement fell into a few core thematic buckets: FOMO (that is, all the cool kids are doing it/using it), humor, desire, fear, and love—you know, the range of emotions you feel every year when you watch Super Bowl ads. Well, I now have a *son* in eighth grade, and not much has changed on the human psychology front.

If I were to sum up my greatest contributions at Sprinkles, beyond the role of founder, it would be as a head of marketing. I am fascinated by the psychology behind human behavior. Perhaps it's because I've had the good fortune to experience so many different places and cultures throughout my life. Regardless, I love trying to find the unifying thread between people, because from my own personal experience, I've seen that we always have more in common than not. (Spoiler alert, this belief relates to Sprinkles' brand vision!)

In this section I will teach you how to position your brand; identify your audience; craft a voice, story, and brand; promise, ideate, and execute a brand identity from scratch; and determine the proper marketing channels for your new business. I can't promise that the hottest Hollywood stars will come flocking, as they did to Sprinkles. But I can promise that you will have a handle on your brand and strategy without having to spend gobs of money on a branding or marketing consultant.

With *your* new business, what's most exciting is that you're starting with a blank slate. *You* get to decide on your logo. *You* get to write the brand promise you always wish you had as a customer. *You* get to determine how to bring your product to market. And once you do, it's time to dream up a PR plan, social media strategy, or community outreach event to get those customers lined up around the block.

So put on your marketer hat and let's get ready to package your idea!

Step Eight

FIND YOUR SPACE
IN THE DISPLAY CASE

Position yourself to differentiate yourself.

For Sprinkles, I didn't have to reach too far to find the target audience. It was me. I was literally customer #1 in those early days, creating for one person and one person only. I was a thirtysomething woman who wanted a freshly baked treat that felt special enough for my own personal enjoyment, celebrations, and gifts. Chances are, you're also building a product that you would buy, so thinking of yourself as the target customer makes it easy to have somewhere to start when it comes to considering your audience's motivations and purchasing behavior.

Still, I did my research. As I visited bakeries around town, I quickly noticed that freshness and presentation were hardly ever a priority. At cafes across LA, I would point to a cookie in the jar and ask when it had been baked. The front counter person either couldn't tell me, or the answer was yesterday or a couple of days ago. I couldn't believe this was accepted as the norm! I knew my standard of same-day freshness would set me apart from other shops in town.

My market research also revealed a surprisingly active culture of gifting among LA professionals. Gifting is standard practice and driven by the entertainment industry's etiquette with one another. People were always looking for chic and thoughtful gifts beyond the usual flowers or candles. I knew if Sprinkles could tap into this market—become a sought-after gift to give and receive—that we would be filling a need for influential people who would become our inadvertent brand ambassadors just by sending our cupcakes as gifts.

UNDERSTAND THE APPETITE

If you know your target audience—where they live, where they shop, and what their interests are—it becomes much easier to continue to create and innovate with this specific person in mind. Again, in my case it was second nature! The key is to own a niche from the beginning; even if you think your company could take over the world someday, no company ever starts out that way. Facebook started as an online directory for a select group of colleges. Uber started as an alternative to hiring a black car. For both tech giants, their devoted group of users helped spread the word and fuel growth because these companies were speaking so clearly to their earliest adopters. Sure, their target market now is literally anyone, but when they were starting out, it was a different story. It was a very specific person, and those founders knew how to speak to them.

Take Katie Warner Johnson, founder of Carbon38, for example. She knew exactly who her customers were—the women who took her Physique 57 classes when she was an instructor. This fitness trainer turned sports bra mogul wanted to disrupt the women's athletic wear industry and did just that by creating a place where she wanted to shop. Her idea was simple: fashion-forward activewear designed by women for women. Johnson always preferred fitness apparel from small, independent, female-led clothing labels, and she wanted to make the products she loved available to a mass audience. In doing so, she also hoped to disrupt the world of athletic wear, which she views as a male-dominated business that markets its products to women. Eventually, the company went on to launch its own line, which now accounts for a third of its business.

As with both Katie and me, sometimes knowing your target audience and place in the marketplace can feel intuitive or empirical based on your own instinct and observations. But if you're a data person, you will want to gather some more statistics and evidence before launching your own line.

YOU WON'T BE TO EVERYONE'S TASTE

Knowing who you're for also means knowing who you're not for. This can be hard, particularly in the service industry where the customer is always right. On top of being a new business owner who wanted to make as many sales as possible, I am also a people pleaser, which made it very difficult to turn customers away. But it's okay to not be right for everyone. For us, we were never going to be the right destination for chronic dieters and calorie counters. There was nothing low-carb about Sprinkles, and that's just how I wanted it to be. LA was full of juice bars, açai bowls, and macrobiotic menus—there were plenty of options for the non-Sprinkles customer.

That said, while I knew people loved a treat, I was also acutely aware of the guilt that can all too often come with eating dessert. To this end, I knew that when people did choose to splurge, they wanted it to feel worth it. Trust me, I had plenty of friends who ate salads so they could justify a cookie at the end of lunch. And holding out for that special moment means something. There is nothing sadder than a disappointing dessert—I mean, what's the point? If I was going to tuck into a long-awaited treat at the end of a meal, it'd better be fresh, delicious, decadent, and satisfying.

Let's be clear: I was raised in the golden era of the low-fat treat. My generation used to eat an entire box of SnackWell's no-fat cookies and think they were absolved of any calories. Why did we eat the whole box? Aside from the misleading marketing that they were "guilt free," the product was so stripped of fat and flavor, and pumped with unpronounceable ingredients, there was no satisfaction. A cupcake is by no means healthy food, but it is *real* food. The cupcake itself is inherently portion-controlled, and my simple, high-quality recipes satisfied. When people came in asking about calories, we reminded them that this was a treat to be enjoyed. We didn't even have the calorie count of cupcakes at the time! Moreover, the act of counting calories wasn't within the Sprinkles ethos. Some people refused to buy one without that information, but that was okay. These weren't our customers.

> When you seek to engage with everyone, you rarely delight anyone. When you zero in and own what you do and speak pointedly to a small group of people, it will resonate with them so strongly that they will help spread your message to the rest of the world. But, going out too wide and trying to be all things to all people is something that no one gets truly excited about. The irony is that the more specific and niche you go, the greater your impact will be.
>
> —*Seth Godin, entrepreneur, bestselling author, and speaker*

FIND YOUR FLAVOR AND STICK WITH IT

Allow me to fast-forward a few years. We're sitting around the family dinner table trying to encourage our seven-year-old son, Harry, to eat broccoli. His brother loved broccoli, but this kid wouldn't budge. We tried to explain how healthy vegetables were, that broccoli was chock-full of vitamins and really delicious. Harry looked up at us and said very matter-of-factly, "Well, everyone has different taste buds." It has since become a family mantra, and it always reminds me of an important lesson in the service business. Despite your best intentions, you can never please everyone.

When we opened Sprinkles, we sold one thing: cupcakes. And so we were able to own that niche. Countless people asked us to add to the product line. "Why can't you do muffins or donuts?" "Make cakes—it's the same batter, how hard could it be?" But when you try to be everything to everyone, you lose your identity. That's dangerous. Know your mission, what you're about, and stick to it—especially in the beginning. Later, when you're more established, you can survey the landscape and spot new areas of opportunity that make sense for the brand and business. For us, we stayed true to cupcakes as our core offering for years. Eventually, once we gained enough clout and loyalty, we were able to expand into cakes, cookies, and even ice cream.

At the same time, you also must know when to let go of what's not working, even if it is part of your brand. When we opened Sprinkles, I had already been creating cupcakes out of my house for a couple of years, so I had a small but loyal following of people who loved my cupcakes and equally loved my custom-made, hand-molded cupcake decorations. I made a wide array of thematic fondant decorations for baby and bridal showers. It was creative and fun, and it filled a need.

But once we opened our store, we could barely bake the cupcakes fast enough to feed people, much less handle custom decorations. I remember the day that Charles came in, as I was hunched over furiously making bespoke decorations, and he said, "We can't offer these anymore." I took one look at the lines of customers waiting for their cupcakes, and I knew he was right. Offering the custom decorations was getting in the way of a larger business.

The people pleaser in me was distraught that I would be letting all those early customers down. But Sprinkles had evolved into something much larger. The move away from ultra-personalization was integral to allowing our business to streamline and scale. It may have been hard, but it was critical to put a stake in the ground and signal to the world what Sprinkles was, who it was here to serve, and who it wasn't. Saying goodbye to fully customized decorations also meant letting go of many wedding, themed party, and shower orders, but the vast majority of people who were lining up simply wanted a cupcake, and they deserved our focus.

BUILD YOUR BRAND POSITIONING STRATEGY FROM SCRATCH

Brand positioning describes how a brand is different from its competitors and where, or how, it sits in customers' minds. Brand positioning allows a company to differentiate itself from competitors, which helps increase brand awareness, communicate value, and justify pricing, all of which impact the bottom line.

Determine your current brand positioning.

Are you currently marketing your product or service as just another item on the market, or are you marketing it as something distinctive? For Sprinkles, we were introducing a totally new concept, so we positioned ourselves as first to market. But here are other ways to position your brand aside from novelty:

- Price: Are you introducing a more affordable option?
- Convenience: Are you creating an easier way to do something?
- Quality: Are you producing something that solves the problem better than anyone else?

Zero in on your target audience.

Your target audience refers to the specific group of consumers most likely to want your product or service and, therefore, the group of people who should see your marketing and branding efforts. Target audience may be dictated by age, gender, income, location, interests, or myriad other factors.

For us, since we were a retail store, we had to find the right real estate for foot traffic. We had a hunch that our customers were tourists who visited Rodeo Drive, and many wanted to take home a piece of the Beverly Hills lifestyle but couldn't afford a memento from one of its designer stores. They could, however, afford a $3 cupcake and enjoy a literal taste of that "rich and famous" lifestyle. As such, we pinpointed a location that was a couple of blocks away—easy walking distance but at a much lower price per square foot than the tony real estate on Rodeo.

For some, you might be looking for your customers online. Either way, you must have a sense of what else your customers are doing (that is, their interests, what else they buy, and where they shop) so you can position yourself near these tangential brands, or even collaborate or partner with them. For instance, we knew our customers also shopped at Williams Sonoma, where we later launched a line of cupcake mixes, and they also watched Food Network, the network that aired my long-running show, *Cupcake Wars*.

Identify and analyze your competitors.

After analyzing your own business, it's important to research your competition by performing a competitor analysis. Who are your direct competitors? With Sprinkles, we had none since we were building something distinct and new, so we looked at the larger market, our indirect competition. These were businesses that weren't necessarily selling the same product but perhaps something similar, including full-scale bakeries and those that created other affordable treats, celebration products, and popular gift items. Even though we weren't in direct competition with some of these businesses, they did offer an alternative option for our customer, and we wanted to be aware of the other choices in the market to position ourselves accordingly.

You'll also need to analyze how your competition is positioning their brand to compete.

- What products or services do your competitors offer?
- What are their strengths and weaknesses?
- What marketing strategies are they using successfully?
- What is their position in the current market?

Be a customer of the competition. Become loyal patrons to your competitors. It's the only way to get to know them enough to be able to differentiate yourself. Investors say that new businesses should be offering a ten-times advantage over the competition. In other words, if you are doing something that already exists, it had better be ten times better than what's out there. The best place to start is to know what's out there, so you can make it better.

I did bakery crawls in various cities. Bakeries, cafes, high-end cake shops: I went anywhere that was serving up anything that closely resembled a cupcake. One New York City bakery crawl left my hotel room littered with dozens of cupcakes, single bites removed, boxes strewn everywhere. It looked like the aftermath of a kid's birthday party, attended by picky eaters. Did all this "market analysis" make me feel mildly ill at times? Well, yes. But it was valuable for me to understand what existed in the current market so I could be confident in the value proposition my product offered.

Create your positioning statement.
A positioning statement is a one- or two-sentence declaration that communicates your brand's unique value to your customers in relation to your main competitors. Answer these four questions before creating your positioning statement:

- Who is your target customer?
- What's your product or service category?
- What's the greatest benefit of your product or service?
- What's the proof of that benefit?

An easy place to start is by filling in the blanks to this statement:

Unlike our competitors who _____ , we do _____ .

FOOD FOR THOUGHT

Defining who you are in the marketplace is a critical step to launching your product onto the scene. Before moving forward with your marketing plan, make sure you can answer these questions:

Who is your target customer? Who isn't your customer?

Have you studied the competitive landscape?

How are you differentiated from the current competition? What is your advantage?

Step Nine

INJECT WITH FILLING

Build a beloved brand.

remember the first time I saw a Sprinkles shopping bag in the wild. It was in the airport! Someone was cradling the large kraft brown paper bag protectively as they went through security and fielding envious comments from TSA. "Ooooh . . . You shouldn't have," joked one of the security agents. Those cupcakes were clearly en route to another part of the country. Perhaps to a recipient who had tasted Sprinkles before and wanted more, or maybe someone who had heard of us and was desperate to see what the fuss was all about. Regardless, when I witnessed those Sprinkles on their way to a faraway destination—and coveted by airport security—it all felt surreal, like an out-of-body experience. I imagine it's a similar experience to how fashion designers feel when they first see someone wearing their clothes on the street, or when a musician first hears their song on the radio.

But that moment was more than just an ego trip for me. It was the moment that I realized Sprinkles was more than its product. It was a recognizable, desirable, certifiable *brand*! I had always known Sprinkles' best offense would have to be its brand because a cupcake is inherently generic, but even I was surprised by how quickly it captured the hearts of consumers everywhere. It was an exciting phenomenon and would prove to be a critical component to our competitive advantage.

As you don your marketing hat, keep in mind that the most important part of your marketing plan is the brand. It needs to be memorable, unique, and authentic. It will be the core of your marketing and advertising strategy, so it needs to be solid to keep all the moving parts together. A brand extends far beyond any visual mark. It's about what your company stands for and how it lives in the perception of your customers.

At Sprinkles, our brand promise was to offer a piece of joy and unity in a tumultuous and fractured cultural climate. And we delivered on that brand promise in so many ways. The brand began and ended with the cupcakes, how they tasted (totally yum), how they were made (fresh each day), how they were decorated (hand frosted, topped with signature decorations), how they were displayed (in a case designed specifically for cupcakes) and how they were packaged (natural, kraft boxes with a pop of pink inside). When a brand is good, there's no break from it. Brand is inherent in every customer touchpoint, and brand manifests in everything that you do as an entrepreneur. It's your guiding North Star.

MAKE YOUR CUSTOMERS SAY "I DO"

Trust in the Sprinkles brand is what allowed Sprinkles to play a role in the most important moments of our customers' lives. Despite discontinuing customized decorations early on, Sprinkles has been the wedding cake option of choice for countless couples. Sprinkles has also played an integral role in many proposals. On one occasion, our team was responsible for stuffing the engagement ring, wrapped in parchment paper, inside the center of a red velvet cupcake before frosting it. When the couple came in to buy their red velvet shortly thereafter, our manager handed the unsuspecting bride the diamond ring–stuffed cupcake. All went well—she said yes, and she didn't break a tooth! On another occasion, the Cupcake ATM was used in a proposal, and again the Sprinkles team was central to the planning of this unique proposal. If you're curious to see how it went down, you're in luck. You can watch the Sprinkles Cupcake ATM proposal on YouTube! Spoiler alert, when the shocked woman opens the box to find a ring inside, she wipes away tears of joy and asks, "But where's my cupcake?"

WHY DOES BRAND TAKE THE CAKE?

I've always admired brands that were able to become so recognizable that they assimilated into our vocabulary. Have a cold? Let me grab you a Kleenex. Can you put the leftovers in a Tupperware? Witnessing someone use *Sprinkles* as a term for all cupcakes might have been the moment I knew I'd really made it.

However, before you set your sights on joining the English dictionary, remember that a brand's main job is to help your product stand out from the crowd and make it easier to earn customer trust. Building a brand is the best thing you can do to differentiate your product. We live in a world where you can buy almost any product—at an insanely low price—at the press of a button from Amazon, which makes competing on price virtually impossible.

So in this global economy, where everything has become commoditized, how do you win over customers? The key is brand. We make decisions all day long based on brand, which brands we want to align ourselves with, and how those brands make us feel. We gravitate toward brands with clear, consistent identities and messages because that reliability across all touchpoints instills a sense of trust, which in turn evolves into loyalty.

WHAT ARE THE MAIN INGREDIENTS FOR A BRAND?

Believe it or not, there was a time when I thought having a great brand just meant having a winning logo and a great business card. Yes, before our iPhone contacts, there were business cards, and they were a big deal. In my investment banking days, Rolodexes were prized possessions. They had a prime spot on every banker's desk and were obsessively updated, culled, and organized. It made sense; these cards were precious relationships, and this was the best way to organize them at the time. But judging a brand by its logo alone is like assuming someone can understand exactly who you are simply by looking at your outfit. Sure, we signal aspects of our personality and value system with the choices we display to the world, but it's only one fraction of the overall picture. The word *brand* gets thrown around a lot, and the meaning can get obscured and diluted. Visual marks such as a business card or logo are in fact part of the visual identity of a brand, but your brand as a whole goes much deeper than that.

> It's important to realize that brand is much more than
> a logo and slogan. A brand is who your company is:
> how you function and make decisions.
>
> —*Joanna McFarland, cofounder of HopSkipDrive*

Look beyond the need your business is filling to get to the emotional reason why people will care. Emily Heyward, founder of marketing agency Red Antler and author of *Obsessed*, calls it "the Why test" and likens it to being the toddler who keeps asking "why" after every answer you give. I've been through this developmental stage with both of my children; it can be annoying, but it does help you get to the simplest explanation for anything in record time. As an entrepreneur, you must ask yourself why your product exists and keep asking until you have laid bare the truest, deepest insight possible. In Sprinkles' case, our why was to help people feel connected to joyful moments and memories with every bite. Jamie Lee Curtis told me once that our banana cupcake was reminiscent of a banana cake she used to eat as a little girl. I would venture to guess that it transported her back to a happy time with a family member she loved. Love and connection: a real why.

Families would come in to celebrate birthdays, of course, but also to mark life's many large and small occasions, such as getting a great grade on a report card, landing a part after a killer audition, or getting a promotion at work. They also came in to make themselves feel better over a lost iPhone or bad breakup. Whatever the situation, happy or sad, Sprinkles elevated the good feelings and made each experience more palatable—literally!

The best place to start when you're building a brand is the foundation. Here are the key elements you'll need to establish before you can even think about logos, fonts, and colors. These will become the fundamental principles that guide every subsequent brand choice.

CRAFT A BRAND BIBLE FROM SCRATCH

Vision

Your brand's vision is about where your company is going and what it is striving for—your reason for being beyond selling a product. Your vision statement should articulate a hope for a future world, made better by what you have created. For Sprinkles it was "A world of unity—a place where people can come together."

The vision can sometimes be difficult to define because it's more conceptual. Oftentimes, it won't become fully clear until you establish other parts of your brand. Allow yourself time to come back at the end if it's not landing right away. A helpful statement to inspire your vision is "Our brand envisions a world where _____ is possible."

Mission

Your mission is your reason for existing today and gives your brand emotional resonance by connecting what your company does with the impact it intends to make. A mission statement will clearly define your business's purpose, objectives, and approach and will act as a compass to keep you marching toward your goals.

My mission at Sprinkles was to deliver joy and connection through food. I did that by creating the best cupcakes in beautiful environments with memorable customer service. What is your mission? How are you delivering on that mission in what you do? How are you communicating that mission consistently through your brand?

Values

Your brand values will communicate what you believe in, what matters most, and the hills you're ready to die on. Having a set moral compass will allow your brand to navigate a changing cultural, social, and economic landscape while remaining true to your original ideals. For Sprinkles, we valued customer joy above all else, providing an unparalleled workplace for our employees and giving back to our community. Knowing, and sticking to, our core values allowed us to find our people and stay the course over time, no matter what changed around us.

For instance, I always believed in the power of cupcakes to sweeten someone's day, whether that person was a customer, employee, or member of the surrounding community who needed some help. We donated daily leftovers to food banks and contributed 100 percent of the proceeds from our charitable cupcakes to causes in which we felt invested, such as our Women's Cancer Research Fund pink ribbon cupcake (which was our pink-hued strawberry cupcake, of course!). These efforts enabled us to give millions in cash and cupcakes to charities and allowed us to connect more deeply to the communities that gave us so much.

Promise

A brand promise sets a clear expectation for your customer about what they will receive from the product and company. It will hold you accountable and set the bar by which you can measure performance. If you notice challenges in demand or customer satisfaction, it's helpful to be able to go back and ask if you're still delivering on that promise.

At Sprinkles, our brand promise was to offer a tangible piece of joy. No matter what kind of day you were having, you could expect to be delighted and satiated. To ensure that we could keep that promise, we empowered our employees to make sure customers were happy, and we owned our channels—always saying no to wholesale—to maintain control over the product, experience, and brand from beginning to end.

BRAND PROMISE, INTERRUPTED.

F act of life: you're not always going to deliver on your brand promise. I remember one busy day at Sprinkles, long before we offered curbside pickup, one of our most beloved and regular customers called to see if someone could run her cupcake order out to her car. She was parked right out front of the bakery on little Santa Monica Boulevard, a busy and particularly narrow thoroughfare. Our manager informed her the store was too busy for anyone to leave, so our customer opened the door to her car to get out and retrieve her cupcakes at the exact moment that a car came speeding by and swiped it clear off! Thank goodness she was uninjured, but the same could not be said for her automobile. This was not the experience I had envisioned for any Sprinkles customer—this was the antithesis of joy. I knew I needed to come up with a solution to make customers' lives easier and keep delivering on our brand promise.

SOURCE YOUR INGREDIENTS

In addition to a brand bible, you're going to need an origin story. Most memorable brands have a compelling backstory that helps bring a human connection to the business. People make purchases with emotion and rationalize with information and logic. If you can't capture their hearts first, you've lost your greatest chance at getting people's attention.

TELL YOUR STORY

N yakio Grieco, cofounder of Thirteen Lune, a diverse beauty platform featuring products by both inclusive brands and Black and Brown founders from around the globe that create products for people of all colors, agrees that an origin story is key to helping a brand resonate with its customers. "People buy into people before they buy into products." Storytelling plays a central role at Thirteen Lune, where they actively spotlight the founder stories of more than one hundred beauty brands through their social media channels and website. "We have curated the most amazing group of storytellers with rich history . . . really celebrating the beauty of inclusion with nontoxic, efficacious, incredible products. It's about discovery and really bringing us all together, unifying us through the lens of beauty," says Nyakio.

Your narrative isn't just a spiel that ends up buried on your company's website. It needs to be a living, breathing story. For instance, Charles and I stood behind that cupcake counter and shared our journey with customers all day long. We told them about how we left our high-paying banking and tech jobs in San Francisco, scared to leave such stable careers, but determined to take a risk to pursue something we were passionate about.

Customers proved to be very curious! "Where did you come from? Did you work in restaurants before this? Are these your grandmothers' recipes?" People liked the product so much that they wanted to know more. They didn't just crave the cupcakes; they also craved a connection to the brand. When they heard our origin story, they felt included in the journey, being able to have a sense of ownership in the success of our business. Over the years, countless customers have excitedly expressed their early discovery of Sprinkles, claiming they were our #1 customer, that they had ordered the most cupcakes, or that they had told the most people about this special new bakery. Early adopters were eager to stake their claim to our brand story, wanting credit for being first on the scene. They were proud of the role they had played in helping tell and shape the Sprinkles journey—and rightfully so! We would have been nothing without their fervent support and brand evangelism.

The most important aspects of our origin story were that it was transparent, authentic, and simple. Our story touched people emotionally and it was also easy enough to spread. Word of mouth is the holy grail of marketing; when you get organic reach from people telling everyone they know, as Sprinkles did, you'll know you have traction. But, for people to share something with someone else, it has to be simple to relay and easy to understand—no matter how technical or obscure the business. Our product was easy to understand, but if yours is harder to articulate, you'll need to do extra work to distill its essence. If someone can't easily explain what you do, you're losing out on your best source of marketing.

And, if *you* can't explain what you do, how will anyone else?

FOOD FOR THOUGHT

Consumers are often drawn into a product by the story behind the product just as much as by as the product itself. Let these questions guide your "Origin Story Checklist":

WHAT was the problem you set out to solve?

WHO was involved?

WHERE did it all go down?

WHEN did inspiration strike?

HOW did it all come together?

WHY was this the moment and WHY were you the perfect person to do this?

Step Ten

GET READY TO DECORATE

Create a compelling brand identity.

A large oil painting was the first purchase I made with my investment banking signing bonus check after graduating college, although I didn't yet have any furniture for my apartment. The irony that I would make such a financially irresponsible decision upon signing on for a job in finance is not lost on me. (Then again, I think I've established that I was never really the best fit for that job.) The purchase spoke to one of my true passions: art and design. As I mentioned before, I grew up in a family that loved collecting. True, the large-scale Asian antiques they accumulated didn't appeal to my specific aesthetic, but the appreciation for art, design, and quality craftsmanship was in my blood.

Naturally I wanted Sprinkles' brand identity to reflect the value I placed on great design. But because Charles and I were bootstrapping this whole business ourselves, we didn't have the budget to hire a big branding agency to create our logo and brand identity. We initially relied on our network and personal connections to help wherever possible—everyone had a friend of a friend who made websites or could do graphic design—and we bounced around to a few before realizing we needed someone to really own the process. We landed at a small design firm in Venice that was up for the challenge, and together, along with our creative consultant, we navigated through the intensive process. As it turns out, creating art is a lot harder than merely being a patron of it!

At the same time, securing a great location in a tight real estate market was proving difficult. So, as the search for our first location dragged on, we spent a lot of time exploring, working on, and ultimately perfecting our brand's look and feel. We took our time to get it right because we could. And, looking back all these years later, that extra time made all the difference in the result. When we set out to build our brand identity, we knew we wanted a logo that captured the nostalgic, timeless comfort of a baked good, while highlighting a more sophisticated and modern aesthetic. Since we had some idea of the creative direction, we figured it wouldn't be too hard to execute the perfect logo.

Turns out, we were a little naive about the design process. You should know right now: a logo is never just a logo. For us, it was a veritable design voyage requiring countless meetings as we pored over Pantone colors, varying line thicknesses, obscure inspiration from organic materials, historical art references, and everyday objects. I could have gotten lost in the minutiae forever. Sure, my past life in banking had left me deft at details, as they pertained to spreadsheets, but this visual world of intricate elements gave me a whole new appreciation for the world of design.

I remember being eager to just be finished, but in retrospect I understand why so much care was given to every inch of our logo. It's truly timeless and has served the brand for nearly two decades. The script of the brand name is not only beautiful, but also speaks to the artisanal, handcrafted quality of our cupcakes. The blocky, modern, frills-free font chosen for *cupcakes* shows our modern attitude and aesthetic. And the iconic dot over the *i* of *Sprinkles* brings a sense of playfulness that ties into the signature cupcake dot decoration that has become synonymous with Sprinkles Cupcakes.

ADD DÉCOR TO THE DECORATING

I had worked long and hard on recipe development and was proud of my product. And in my quest to reinvent the cupcake, it became clear to me that my premium product needed to be supported with an equally upscale environment. Think about it: I had created a luxury product with the world's finest and most expensive vanilla and chocolate. Everything surrounding the product also needed to reflect how special it was, starting with our location. We ultimately landed a spot in Beverly Hills. Sure, it was the size of a postage stamp, measuring six hundred square feet for both front and back of house, and it wasn't Rodeo Drive, it was "Rodeo Drive–adjacent." But the famous zip code was a signal to the world about the artisanal product we were creating and the superior experience we were providing. Moreover, just like the shops a couple of blocks over on Rodeo Drive, our boutique would sell something handcrafted and hard to get your hands on. Everything about the product, packaging, and presentation had to look expensive.

Every element of this new treat and its environment had to be imagined and then rethought and reimagined once more. Like I've said before, cupcakes needed a makeover. They were a treat made for kids and typically found either in supermarkets or in bakeries that looked like your grandma's kitschy kitchen—you know, vintage fifties-style mixers, frilly aprons, and doilies. While I was ready to lose Nana's wholesome retro image, I did want to keep the nostalgic taste and feel of the cupcake. By upgrading this grade-school treat and making it more sophisticated, I knew I could increase the potential market beyond kids and their lunchboxes. Cupcakes had always been cutesy, even girlish—with pastel-colored sprinkles and cupcake wrappers. But I wanted to bring this sweet treat into the modern day with a gender-neutral aesthetic that would appeal to everyone at any age.

We turned our attention to the store design. As it turns out, transforming an old sandwich shop into our glistening cupcake bakery vision cost us $200,000—a staggering number given our tiny footprint. It was *way* more than we had ever imagined or budgeted for it to cost and we knew we would have to value engineer future locations, but this flagship spot had to be just right. We invested in an amazing architect and designer—both had a clean, modern eye. Every detail was carefully considered—no doilies! The bakery had to be a space women *and* men found joyful. The result was a store that combined the warmth of finished woods and natural light with the modern look of glass and steel and playful punches of color.

One thing that irked us about existing bakeries is the way products—and in particular cupcakes—were displayed. They were typically lined up in prefabricated display cases that were low to the ground and unorganized in messy pushed-together trays. This presentation, where the unappetizing wrapper profile was front and center, made it difficult for customers to be drawn to the product. We enlisted the incredible talent of our architect, Andrea Lenardin Madden of ALM Project, to help design the perfect display case to show off our little beauties. This included trays that slid in and out with die-cut holes where each cupcake would sit. This meant that, regardless of an employee's attention to detail, the cupcakes would always sit in a perfect line. The sliding trays also made restocking a breeze because employees didn't have to reach inside static display cases. Our new displays sat tall and positioned the cupcakes at eye level with a slight angle to capture the prettiest part of the cupcake: its top! When you walked in our store, you were immediately struck by the vision of rows upon rows of cupcakes in perfect file, flaunting luscious frosting, pretty sprinkles, and colorful decorations.

DECONSTRUCTING THE CUPCAKE

It was important for a Sprinkles Cupcake to be truly distinctive, to set it apart from the pack. Aside from a unique and elevated cake recipe on the inside, I wanted the outside aesthetic to stand out in a big way, so I focused on three areas: frosting, wrappers, and decorations.

Most bakeries use piping bags to frost cupcakes because it's fast and easy, but the uniform result is something reminiscent of a factory line product. However, with an offset spatula, I was able to make the frosting look smooth and elegant, yet still handcrafted, applied generously across the top of the cake so that every bite had an equal and ideal frosting-to-cake ratio. This was opposed to the piping bag aesthetic of the time, which left the perimeter of the cake bare and piled the middle with an uneven heap of frosting. The technique is what we now call "the Sprinkles swirl." Frosters at our bakery practice on *thousands* of cupcakes to perfect the swirl. It's not easy, but it is beautiful!

And, while most bakeries used the standard white or pastel-colored wrappers, I opted for chocolate brown cupcake wrappers. Not only did they feel more elegant, but their opaqueness hid any imperfections in the cake. They also lent a gravitas to the cupcakes, unifying and grounding them en masse so that the cupcakes didn't feel too busy, allowing the most aesthetically pleasing part of the cupcake—the frosting and decorations on top—to pop.

Of course, the most iconic part of a Sprinkles Cupcake is the bright, fun sugar design that features two concentric circles we call modern dots. I wanted to create a new type of "sprinkle" to match the modern nature of a Sprinkles Cupcake. I had reinvented the cupcake, so why not turn the topping upside down, too? I needed to create a differentiating mark, so if there was a buffet table of desserts, the Sprinkles would be instantly recognizable and distinct from the rest. Initially, all the modern dots were made by hand in the bakery and topped cupcakes randomly, but the problem was that when customers took home their cupcakes, they didn't know which cupcake was which. Shortly after opening, we decided to assign a certain dot to each flavor to give customers a guide, like the way flourishes help distinguish truffles from caramels in a box of chocolates. We also realized that hand-making all the decorations was extremely laborious and a hindrance to productivity, so we decided to outsource this aspect. And thankfully, in time we were able to trademark the modern dot, which helped us protect ourselves in what became a sea of copycat competitors.

But doing everything made-to-order was unrealistic. When it came to packaging, a custom box would require a huge minimum run and a big investment. At that time, there were no cupcake boxes in production aside from plastic clamshells, which clearly wasn't going to work for us. So we got scrappy. To keep packaging costs low, but still on brand, we took standard pink cake boxes and turned them inside out to make them our own. They were kraft brown on the outside and, upon opening, revealed a pop of pink that was the perfect backdrop to the cupcakes inside. It was important to us that this new-millennium take on a classic comfort food extended from our cupcake design to our storefront aesthetic and all the way through to the packaging.

PUT YOUR BEST FACE FORWARD

Think of identity as the face of a brand. While the brand itself is an emotional, and even philosophical, concept, identity is the visual component that represents those larger ideas through specific visual and messaging cues.

A brand identity includes logos, typography, colors, packaging, and messaging, which should all complement and reinforce the existing reputation of a brand. Brand identity provides both customer acquisition and retention. It will attract new customers to your brand, while also reinforcing your brand values and mission with loyal, existing customers.

It's important that brand identity be consistent, which is why it's often referred to as a "brand identity system." The message portrayed by brand identity components, both visual and written, needs to be clear and the same no matter where it's displayed—from business card to packaging and every digital channel. Think of it as presenting a united front!

BUILDING A BRAND IDENTITY FROM SCRATCH

Logo

Which came first—the logo or the brand? In Sprinkles' case, and in most situations, a clear brand comes first, followed by a logo that matches, complements, and enhances that brand.

Your logo is central to your brand identity design. It's the piece of your brand identity that people will be exposed to first and most often. It needs to line up with all the other elements of your brand identity as well as the broader emotional appeal of your brand.

Color

The colors that represent your brand are what make your brand instantly recognizable. Take Coca-Cola for example. You'd be hard-pressed to find anyone that didn't associate red and white with the global, household brand. With Sprinkles, brown and pink were our chosen signature colors. The brown was inspired by the color of chocolate, which also informed our unique brown cupcake wrappers. The pink spoke to the confectionary nature of cupcakes, but pinpointing the perfect hue was quite a task. We didn't want a harsh-looking "Barbie pink"; it had to be something warmer—and a color we could really own.

To ensure that everyone uses the correct color throughout all possible communications, we don't say our brand colors are pink and brown. Rather, we assign CMYK and PMS color codes for print, and RGB for digital media. Sprinkles pink is PMS 197 and Sprinkles brown is PMS 175.

Typography

Typography is one of the most overlooked aspects of design, but it has the power to convey so much. The fonts you use to communicate your brand can say even more than the words themselves. The look and feel of the typography make an immediate impression on people, before they even have time to read the words—not to mention having an impact, even if you don't have the ability to understand the language. When you're choosing a typeface, there are broad general categories, such as script, sans serif, serif, and blackletter, that all evoke a different mood, tone, and message. From there you can consider the weight (thin, semi-bold, bold, extra bold), spacing, and capitalization.

Something in script might feel fancy, delicate, or sophisticated. A typeface with serifs feels official or institutional—think *The New York Times*. Meanwhile, something without serifs might feel more modern, as we chose with Sprinkles—an important message we wanted to convey about our product through visual brand identity. And that's only if you're deciding to go with a typeface that already exists. You can also work with a designer to make modifications or create a completely custom typeface—a huge undertaking. No matter what you choose, every decision you make about your typeface needs to support your brand messaging.

Brand Usage

Once you've determined the core elements of your brand identity, establish clear brand guidelines in a brand style guide. As your brand grows, other brand partnerships, PR reps, and media will want access to your branding for various purposes. The style guide should provide clear direction on how your logo, brand colors, and typography should be used in all these cases.

Remember, the details count! You can't expect people to represent your brand correctly if you are lax with the details.

Visual Attributes

Your brand doesn't just stop at its logo. Your brand should have a look, feel, and visual identity that helps customers recognize and connect with it across touchpoints—from in store to website to digital ads and social media channels.

It helps to put your brand's visual identity into words. What mood, feeling, or emotions should your brand elicit from your audience? Be descriptive and provide examples of appropriate visuals. Also, a picture is worth a thousand words: Mood boards are a great way to provide inspiration and guidance for different expressions of the brand.

Voice

Brand voice is the distinct personality a brand takes on in its communications, across all channels. From signage, print, digital, and social, this personality will express itself a little differently depending on the platform. Just as individuals present themselves differently in various situations and environments, a brand voice will act the same.

Who is your brand online? If your brand were a person, what personality traits would they take on, and what would they actively avoid? What phrases and stylistic choices does your brand use on a consistent basis? This personality is applied everywhere your brand speaks, including newsletters, social media posts, and advertising—even internal company announcements.

Persona

Brand personality has a huge impact on the voice and tone used in your marketing materials and other communications. If a personality isn't established, customers may get mixed messages and have trouble connecting with your brand.

If you're having a hard time getting started, here's an exercise to try: Which celebrities best represent your brand? Is there an actor or actress, musician, or public personality who embodies the same traits as your brand? This could be a good starting point for nailing down different aspects of your brand's personality.

For Sprinkles, I accidentally became the brand's persona and spokesperson. It was hard to know where Sprinkles started, and I ended. But more on that later . . .

FOOD FOR THOUGHT

When building your brand identity, consider these more abstract ideas to help you arrive at a unique and authentic look and feel:

Which three adjectives best sum up the mood of your brand?

What colors best represent your brand?

Which celebrities embody the same traits as your brand?

If your brand were a person, how would they speak?

Step Eleven

PUT OUT YOUR
SANDWICH BOARD

*Tailor your marketing strategy
to find your customers.*

Moving to Los Angeles to open a bakery, I never expected to become part of the Hollywood scene beyond a celebrity sighting here and there. I came to make cupcakes, not the cover of *People* magazine. But, by choosing our location in Beverly Hills, we knew we would come into direct contact with high-profile customers, fans, and partners. For instance, I was introduced to Henry Winkler (yes, the Fonz!) and his wife, Stacey, through a mutual friend. Stacey was known for being a generous hostess, regularly opening her home to new and old friends. She had a passion for food and was particularly known for her dessert tables piled high with her favorite treats from around LA.

Because Sprinkles became a fixture at these parties, I was invited as a guest, which is where I met Chris McMillan. You may not know his name, but you most assuredly know his work. He is the stylist behind Jennifer Aniston's famous "Rachel" haircut and works with countless other top Hollywood starlets, agents, and even international royalty. It was natural for us to strike up a conversation, both being business owners in Beverly Hills. Chris had an avid sweet tooth and loved Sprinkles, so I obliged my new friend by bringing cupcakes into his salon every week.

Turns out, my instincts for making friends also made for an incredible marketing opportunity. Every single day, the salon was packed with a diverse cross-section of customers, tastemakers, and high-profile clientele with nothing to do while they were there but sit, chat, flip through magazines, and snack. Stylists at the salon were known for being in the know and talked with clients all day long, dishing on what was hot and what was not. The owner's favorite new decadent treat was most definitely *hot,* and word spread through the salon and beyond. In retrospect, this was influencer marketing before *influencer marketing* was even a term.

WHEN YOU RUN OUT OF INGREDIENTS, GET SCRAPPY

Did we pursue this grassroots technique because we were marketing geniuses? No! It was the neighborly thing to do. (Okay, it was also super cheap to harness the power of people and get them talking.) Because our product was unlike anything else available, it gave them something to talk about while waiting for their 2000s en vogue chunky highlights to set.

By the time we were all prepped and ready to put out our sandwich board, we had little money left to put toward marketing. Renovating the space to fit our exact vision had exceeded our budget, and all we were left with was our creativity and plenty of time. That said, we did consider our hefty investment in our brick-and-mortar space to be like an expensive billboard, and we tapped a friend who had worked in magazines and PR to help us draft a press release. That same friend also worked the counter on the weekends. We were scrappy! We pulled in any friend with a bit of free time who wanted to pitch in on the side.

While we had friends and family helping from every angle, we hit the ground—literally. I dragged myself to every single opportunity to spread the word—trunk shows, parties, you name it. I reached out to party planners and worked my entire friend network from the inside out. I had friends with fledgling fashion and jewelry lines who would invite me to trunk shows so I could set up a table with cupcake samples and hand out business cards. I took cupcakes to hotel concierges to make sure they were in the know about our new and uniquely LA destination for them to tell their visiting guests about.

The fact that I had been selling cupcakes out of my apartment before opening a shop meant I already had a small built-in customer base. Much like a company might build a waiting list for a product prelaunch, these customers helped build the buzz and demand before opening day and tipped off the trend-spotting editors at DailyCandy. For those of you who don't remember it, DailyCandy was a beloved, daily email blast on what was new and happening that day in Los Angeles (as well as other major cities across the United States). To be featured in DailyCandy was a highly coveted opportunity; its recommendations were widely followed and greatly trusted. DailyCandy was planning to feature the Sprinkles opening, with their email blast scheduled to coincide with our opening morning. Even though we were desperate to push our opening date by a few days, doing so would have meant losing the story, so we forged ahead. And thankfully so.

The DailyCandy coverage struck a serious chord—curious tastemakers around LA came out in droves to check out this chic, modern, cupcakes-only bakery. It was a concept opposed to everything they knew. Low-carb still ruled the day! And bakeries weren't supposed to be, well, cool! But, as it turns out, sometimes flying in the face of the status quo is inherently newsworthy. It grabs people's attention and gets them talking. And, when people are talking about you, they're doing your marketing for you. (In fact, it worked so well that it meant that we wouldn't have to allocate a budget toward any official marketing for years.) I also learned an early lesson in the almighty power of email marketing.

We sold out within a few hours, leaving me in the kitchen frantically baking for people who were willing to wait for any flavor I pulled from the oven. Cupcakes were going out straight from the oven, and frosting was melting off them like butter on hot toast, but people did not care. They *had* to have them. And the scarcity appeared to be fueling demand even more!

MAKE YOUR HIT A TIMELESS CLASSIC

From a marketing perspective, Sprinkles was an absolute anomaly—true lightning in a bottle. Based on everything we knew about the retail business, we could never have anticipated the velocity at which we expanded, with barely any proactive marketing strategy or tactics in place. No one could have predicted the way in which we were able to grow through word of mouth and then via an unsolicited celebrity-endorsed explosion—all within the first few years.

I remember watching *Live with Regis and Kelly* in amazement one morning in 2008 as Blake Lively shared her passion for Sprinkles and her wish that we would open an outpost in New York City. She had already been a vocal fan at this point, and it occurred to me that Blake needed to have her very own Sprinkles Cupcake. As she was an accomplished chef in her own right, it made so much sense! Later, when we debuted our NYC bakery, I approached her with the idea of creating a new flavor for our menu with proceeds going to support the charity of her choice. Blake was inspired to create not just a delicious new flavor but an experience in a bite. After months of experimenting, the scrumptious s'more cupcake was born, and Blake chose Oxfam, a charity close to her heart, to be the recipient of the proceeds. Fans of both Blake and Sprinkles came out in droves to raise tens of thousands of dollars for Oxfam.

Sprinkles couldn't have asked for a more perfect first celebrity ambassador than the lovely Blake Lively. In fact, the philanthropic partnership was so successful that we continued the celebrity charitable cupcake initiative with other beloved personalities. Over the years, we raised money with Michael Strahan for St. Jude, Drew Barrymore for United Friends of the Children, Jessica Alba for Baby2Baby, Kerry Washington for Americans for the Arts, Ne-Yo for the Compound Foundation, and Tony Hawk for the Tony Hawk Foundation. I had always believed in the power of a cupcake to make good things happen, but this was beyond my expectations. This unique union of celebrity, charity, and cupcake was a powerful win for all and proof that my favorite cake may be small but it was certainly mighty.

Though Sprinkles' word of mouth was supercharged by some bold-faced names, the tactic of leveraging word of mouth is timeless and effective, even in the absence of superstar status. Generally speaking, we listen to the advice and recommendations of people we know, like, and trust the best. It could be a favorite face from the big and small screens, the person sitting next to you at the salon, or, increasingly likely these days, a social media influencer with a LIKEtoKNOW.it account.

HOT TIP

How you plan to get your product into the hands of customers is known in start-up circles as your "go-to market" strategy and it's a critical piece of launching any new business.

There are countless methods for customer acquisition, but the goal is to find the most effective strategy for you. Companies that have a low-cost method for acquiring customers, such as a massive email list or a large and engaged following on social media, have an inherent advantage. As an example, consider the impact of Kim Kardashian posting about her shapewear company, SKIMS, to her hundreds of millions of followers.

TAKE YOUR SIDEWALK SALE INTO THE DIGITAL AGE

It's crazy to me that the term *direct to consumer* (*DTC*) hadn't even been coined when I started Sprinkles, and now there is an entire category of companies forgoing traditional retail distribution models to sell directly to consumers online. Many of these companies are now household names: Warby Parker, Allbirds, and Away are consumer giants whose success can in large part be attributed to the effectiveness of Facebook's advertising platform. As I mentioned, when I first started selling cupcakes, Facebook was still just a website for college elites to connect, and now the ease with which anyone can start an advertising campaign with a few clicks of a button and reach a universe of people has changed the marketing landscape forever. Although the economics of running an online advertising campaign is always in flux, the ease of running a Facebook ad campaign and the targeted nature of Google Ads remains beyond any sort of marketing we could ever have imagined almost twenty years ago.

But blasting ads across the internet is relatively new to the marketing universe, and even if it takes up most of your marketing pie, it won't be the only slice. Beyond the myriad digital channels at our fingertips, there is still plenty more to move the marketing needle. In fact, there are so many marketing channels in today's world that it can feel overwhelming for an entrepreneur just starting out. How do you know where you need to be? How do you know where you *don't* need to be? Everyone's marketing mix is going to look a bit different and will evolve and expand as you grow.

I experienced this firsthand in my post-Sprinkles role as a principal in CN2 Ventures, a venture studio Charles and I founded to incubate new concepts. After years of managing brick-and-mortar stores and a brand that quickly found widespread success, I faced a learning curve as I moved into my role as a partner and investor in several new businesses. From launching and investing in more food concepts like a high-end pizza restaurant and wellness cleanse to partnering on a children's sensory development platform and a DTC men's athleisure line, I've had to add quite a few new skills to my marketing resume.

In these new ventures, the product and landscape were very different from Sprinkles. Though we employed digital marketing across all of these businesses, the mix of marketing channels and levers we pulled for each varied substantially based on the nature of the product and the customer we were targeting. For instance, at CN2 Ventures' pizza concept, Pizzana, we harnessed the power of storytelling across media to share our chef's American Dream origin story, the quality of Pizzana's ingredients, and its artisanal technique. Our children's platform, Play 2 Progress, has thrived by partnering with similarly mission-minded companies in the early childhood space, expanding brand awareness and cultivating new customers by sharing our founder's expert content with their communities. Willy California, our men's apparel line, has utilized content marketing, search engine optimization (SEO), and trunk shows to court the ever-elusive male buyer.

These marketing channels worked because we looked at who our customers were and what would inspire them to try something new—*and this demanded more than a one-size-fits-all strategy.* A notable chef with a great story gave our high-end pizza concept the credibility we needed to tell customers it was LA's hot new dining experience. It made sense that Play 2 Progress would be successful only if parents were on board and talking about it with their friends. And, while we buy clothes online without a second thought, being able to touch and try on items will always seal the deal.

When you're ready to launch your brand, avoid the pressure to be everywhere at once, and focus on who you're trying to reach and what they would need to be convinced to try your product. It always pays (or rather saves) to start small, test, learn, and adjust as you go.

HOW OUR PLACE FOUND A HOME ONLINE

Shiza Shahid was anything but a marketer when she started the direct-to-consumer cookware brand Our Place. Before launching her big idea, Shiza had primarily worked in human rights, building nonprofits like the Malala Fund. Her experience and passion working in impact was a driver in wanting to start Our Place and has become integral to the ethos of the brand. Though far from an experienced marketer, Shiza was a top-notch storyteller.

With this special skill in telling untold, underrepresented stories, Shiza launched Our Place with a clear mission: a desire to bring people together through cooking. In her experience, many marginalized communities do not feel seen by how food is portrayed in media, entertainment, and consumer goods. She wanted to change that with products that represented more than a meal—a brand that welcomed and connected traditions in the kitchen, from all over the world.

When it comes to marketing, Shiza believes that anyone can figure out how to launch a digital marketing campaign, but what you can't Google is an authentic mission. For her, once her brand's mission was solidified, finding the right channels became a game of testing and iterating.

Though they impressively became profitable six months into business, Our Place launched without outside funding and had a limited budget when it came to marketing. Shiza definitely didn't want to throw darts at a wall in the hopes that one would stick. With that in mind, she steered clear of big, flashy television ads with little data and ROI.

Instead, she started small and narrow, by capturing emails, launching an organic Instagram account, and creating authentic, unique content in the hopes of finding their true customer base. At the center of Our Place's marketing and advertising plan was building community. Every tactic had to come back to this goal, and it had to be strategic. To accomplish this, they focused on sharing unique, culturally underrepresented, and nostalgic comfort recipes and images of real tables that felt cozy but not overly styled with inaccessible items. Overall, their marketing set out to make cooking and gathering more accessible and community oriented.

Most digital channels will allow you to spend small amounts to start and immediately adjust or pull back if it's not working. Traditional marketing channels such as television, print, or billboards are more static and require a higher minimum investment. Because the nature of digital marketing offers more flexibility to reach customers at any budget it was a great place for a fledgling DTC brand with a smaller marketing spend to begin.

In addition to a strategic digital plan, Shiza understood the importance of gifting generously. With an intimate, everyday item like cookware, being able to touch, feel, and try the product was imperative, since Our Place was not sold in stores. They were strategic in choosing partners by targeting the everyday people who don't consider themselves to be good cooks. Shiza wanted to be able to gift them a beautiful, special kitchen tool that could empower them not just to make a meal but also tap into their own heritage and culture of cooking.

Just a few years into launch, Our Place is growing exponentially, but starting small, testing, and iterating are still a fundamental way to keep marketing channels focused and effective.

HOW TO START A MARKETING PLAN FROM SCRATCH

Being strategic about where and how your business is being seen by prospective customers is critical. Here are some foundational channels on which you can start to plot your marketing plan. When you're just launching your big idea, there might not be a huge marketing budget to work with. You can always start with one or two channels that make the most sense for your brand and grow as you go.

Build a website.

In today's technology-based world, you need a website to show you're legit and to offer information about your business to potential customers. Assuming you are selling through your site, you'll need one that is optimized for e-commerce (Shopify and Squarespace are great options). Considering that mobile makes up most e-commerce sales, with that percentage only rising, remember to make your site mobile-friendly. There are a ton of do-it-yourself website services, but depending on the features you need on your site, some things are better left to the experts. Although there are platforms, like Upwork and Fiverr, dedicated to finding and hiring tech talent, I always prefer a personal recommendation. Ask your friends and professional network to recommend their favorite freelance web designers.

Drive traffic.

Once you've built your website, the goal is to drive traffic to it! Clearly it helps if your website ranks high among Google's results for keywords. If you are garnering press and your business is generating a lot of "noise," your ranking will increase organically. If your website is still languishing on page 50 of Google results when searching your most meaningful keyword, you might need a little push. There are tactics to employ to improve your ranking, such as creating quality, keyword-rich content that, when linked to by other sites, improves site authority and relevance. There are also plenty of experts who specialize in SEO (search engine optimization) to help drive organic traffic to your site.

Get social.

Let's face it, everyone is on social media these days, and most of the traffic occurs on just a few platforms: Facebook, Instagram, TikTok, YouTube, LinkedIn, and Pinterest, to name a handful of the biggies. These will also become key traffic drivers to your site. Share content that inspires, educates, or entertains. Your social content should resonate and connect with your audience in a way that compels them to act, whether that's a link, a comment, or a share. Build a community by speaking directly to your followers and using it as an opportunity for customer feedback and to collect valuable testimonials. When you authentically build an engaged audience of fans, they will buy whatever you're selling.

Advertise strategically.

The bulk of your advertising efforts will likely live online. This will come from a combination of search advertising on Google and through Facebook's advertiser platform. Search ads on Google will target the types of products or services you offer in specific geographic locations and drive meaningful visitors to your site who are actively seeking your product. Facebook and Instagram or TikTok advertising is a great way to meet your customers where they are already hanging out with ads that look and feel just like the organic content they're consuming.

That said, don't discount the power of direct marketing tactics like mailers, email, and SMS text messages. You should not try all these advertising platforms at once, though! Advertising can very quickly feel like putting precious dollars into a food processor, and you don't want to waste the budget. Pick a few, see how they work, and determine if you want to explore other channels.

Create a buzz.

Your first stop in creating a buzz is your own personal network. Start by building an email list from your contacts. Next, search your contacts for friends in media or PR who could help you get your product into the right hands or get you on a top podcast. Remember that Rolodex I mentioned from my banking days? Now is the time to dust those proverbial cards off and put them to work. Although you will always have more success with your network (warm leads) than complete strangers (cold leads), there is still a small percentage of people who will respond to a stranger. Cold calling can be scary, but it works! In the modern world, cold calling doesn't have to mean picking up the phone (terrifying). Today, you can simply and passively slide into someone's DMs. I get DMs on Instagram all the time from business owners who want to send me their product with the hope that I will share some love on Instagram. And often I say "Sure, send it over!" You're going to need to put your ego aside and ask the favors.

Run promotions and partner with like-minded brands for giveaways online or show up to in-person events to offer samples. A happy customer will come back and will tell their friends about you. Likewise, you can also create buzz with brand ambassadors. Sure, established influencers are great, but these can also be family and friends who help promote your products or services when you're just starting out.

And don't forget to have a presence offline by finding ways to get involved at the local level. Networking is a great way to capture business leads if you don't come on too strong. It allows you to meet new contacts and create more brand awareness and new referrals. Sponsor sporting events, nonprofit events, or anything that is for a good cause. Get your name out there while also being a good community steward.

Hire it out!

Perhaps my best piece of advice is to try not to tackle this all yourself. There's a reason that people do all this stuff for a living. While you'll be running the operation, there's no need to get too in the weeds: A whole universe of experts is eager to guide your marketing spend. If you don't have investor dollars to burn, lean into grassroots, on-the-ground marketing and favors from well-connected friends to use word of mouth to build a buzz. Think: friends who work in media, who have large email lists or social media followings, or who are willing to throw you a party to spread the word. Later, when the cash is flowing, you can hire a public relations and digital marketing agency.

Either way, your best opportunity to get media placements and the public's attention is when your product is new, so put everything you have toward the initial launch. Garnering buzz early on can be critical to kick-start awareness and encourage adoption.

FOOD FOR THOUGHT

From hitting a "like" button to hitting the streets, you can get the word out about your product in many ways. When planning your marketing strategy, ask yourself the following questions:

What is your marketing budget and how do you plan to put it to work?

What mix of grassroots, in-person efforts, or digital marketing makes the most sense for your brand?

Are you prepared to mine your network and call in favors to support your marketing efforts?

How much professional expertise will you need to outsource?

Step Twelve

TAKE OFF THE APRON

Step into the spotlight
and make friends with the lens.

P icture me between rushes at the bakery, only stopping at home to quickly take our dog, Honey, for a walk. As I hurried poor Honey to do her business during my break, my cell phone started blowing up. *Had I seen it? Was I so excited? Could I even believe it?*

The "it" was Katie Holmes gushing about Sprinkles on a national entertainment show during a press junket. She called it her favorite little secret in Beverly Hills. "My mouth is already salivating," Katie said, rather emphatically. No, I couldn't believe it. Our first national exposure was huge, and from the lips of a major celebrity no less? This was beyond my wildest dreams. Not to mention I freaking loved Joey Potter—erm—I mean Katie Holmes. I was (and still am) a diehard *Dawson's Creek* fan.

But beyond WB fame (which was not nothing in the early aughts), this was right about the time she was being pursued by Tom Cruise. Every time this Hollywood legend would send his new crush a box of Sprinkles Cupcakes, it became hot gossip magazine fodder, which was essentially a lot of free national press.

⊙

Stars, they're just like us!
They like to eat cupcakes!

I still don't understand how I found myself swept up in the tornado that was TomKat fever, but the golden couple of the hour had become synonymous with Sprinkles Cupcakes, and we were off to the races. For months, TomKat couldn't get enough of our product, and the media could not get enough TomKat, fighting over each other to grab both of their attention on the red carpet using Sprinkles Cupcakes as bait.

Remember, this was the height of paparazzi chasing starlets like Lindsay Lohan and Britney Spears all over Los Angeles. Paris Hilton celebrated her birthdays with Sprinkles. A photo of Jessica Alba walking out of Sprinkles with her bag of cupcakes was splashed across gossip rags. To put the power of paparazzi as a means of free publicity into perspective, it was widely known that some businesses would court paparazzi, and young stars looking to be photographed, by essentially scheduling a media "event" for the celebrity. Basically, businesses with storefronts would stage a paparazzi sighting by alerting photographers that a star was on their way or already in their store. Sometimes the star was also in on it, somehow perfectly camera-ready for their "candid" shot. It was a boon for all: The photographers would sell their photos to the tabloids, the aspiring star would know they were going to look good in the photo, and the business would get a publicity blast and celebrity association in the weeklies. In short, businesses paid large sums of money to replicate the phenomenon we were experiencing organically. We, on the other hand, were always deflecting paparazzi, wanting to keep Sprinkles a safe space for our household-name clientele, though to be honest we did relish the celebrity attention.

On many occasions, I remember shutting the shade in our big front window to allow privacy from paparazzi cameras on the sidewalk outside. If a celebrity was being harassed, we would help them dodge cameras out front by ushering them through the kitchen and out the back door. But that was the only concierge service we ever offered, and really in the most critical circumstances. Everyone was a VIP at Sprinkles, which meant everyone waited in line—famous people too. No cut-sies! There's an unwritten rule in Hollywood that celebrities never wait in line. Yet, every day we saw highly recognizable faces standing patiently in line for their Sprinkles Cupcakes. We had unintentionally made waiting in line . . . trendy?

THE TIPPING POINT

Several months into the TomKat blitz and eight months after opening, we had just made it through our first holiday season, which was unlike anything we had experienced to date. That holiday season of 2005, Sprinkles Cupcakes was the "gift to give" for many of the top studio execs, agents, producers, and celebs in Los Angeles. We were completely exhausted and looking forward to a little lull in January while everyone was grumbling through their New Year's juice cleanses. It was late afternoon; we had turned off the ovens for the day and were cleaning up when we got a call from Harpo Studios. Yes, as in Oprah. I know everyone likes to claim that they're an Oprah fan, but I really was a mega fan, religiously watching *The Oprah Winfrey Show* for years. She had, after all, inspired me from my couch in San Francisco to get off my tush and into the game. Now, Oprah herself had told the producers she wanted Sprinkles on the show. Could we have 350 cupcakes for their Chicago-based studio audience the next morning? No matter the logistical nightmare that would ensue, there was only one answer: "YES."

"Great, we'll send a courier, who will put them under the plane," replied a Harpo producer matter-of-factly. Though I was in absolute delighted shock, I was present enough to realize that mode of transport would spell disaster for our cupcakes. We didn't ship Sprinkles Cupcakes for a reason, and I knew this arrangement could very quickly flatten our notorious cupcakes into unintentional pancakes. Still, we couldn't miss out on the opportunity of a lifetime.

So, I fired up the ovens and Charles and I booked a red-eye to Chicago, boarding the plane with as many cupcakes as we could carry. We stacked boxes into the largest shopping bags we could find and carried as many as we could, which meant we literally brought nothing else. Thank goodness it was midnight as we went through security because we had to remove every single box of cupcakes from their bag to be sent through the X-ray machine individually. It took *forever*. We repeated the same nerve-wracking choreography as we loaded into the cabin, removing each box and placing it carefully in the overhead compartment. If anyone looked annoyed or frustrated, all we had to do was say the magic words, "We're going to Oprah!" It's amazing how fast that line can turn eye rolls into high-fives.

We arrived before Oprah, just in time to perfectly hand-plate all 350 cupcakes and to catch her walking in for hair and makeup (followed by Mary J. Blige, who was the guest performer that day—as if the day could get any better). Oprah is one of those people who truly take your breath away to see in real life.

As we watched the episode from backstage, we couldn't believe our eyes and ears when Oprah unleashed a veritable love letter to Sprinkles, telling the story of how her friend Barbra Streisand had introduced her to these delicious cupcakes that all the Hollywood stars loved. As we left the studio, the producer told us in a very understated way that we should be prepared for an uptick in business when the show aired. Several weeks later, when it did air, we had a line that wrapped all the way down our block and around the other side. And it remained that way for months. Overnight, our little bakery had become a sensation with brand recognition around the world. The Oprah Effect was incredible: Our sales reached new heights of up to twenty thousand cupcakes a day in Beverly Hills!

This phenomenon wasn't just reflected in our daily sales reports; it was in the zeitgeist. Sprinkles Cupcakes was written into television shows like *Entourage*. In fact, there's a memorable scene in which Ari Gold, bigwig agent, comes rolling through the office boasting, "I brought Cristal and Sprinkles Cupcakes, your favorite." We popped up on the small screen, with a prominent role in *The Girls Next Door*, a reality show about Hugh Hefner's three main girlfriends living it up at the Playboy mansion, and were even mentioned on the big screen in Judd Apatow's *The 40-Year-Old Virgin*.

LEVERAGE YOUR TASTEMAKERS

You wouldn't believe the parade of people who waltzed through our doors in that first year: It ranged from perfectly manicured Beverly Hills socialites to celebrities with full entourages, rock stars, sports greats and top managers, agents, assistants, and even Saudi princesses. Honestly, it was jaw-dropping at the time and remains that way today. We had every studio's holiday list and were on speed dial for all the private plane catering companies. In short, we had a front-row seat to how the 1 percent lived—with cupcakes.

We needed these tastemakers, but also knew they would leave us eventually. LA was littered with the remains of fly-by-night businesses who catered solely to trendsetters, hipsters, and connoisseurs without any thought for the future once they were no longer novel. But even though they were inevitably fleeting, tastemakers are the ultimate social proof.

We'd been in LA long enough to know this first wave of fans was going to be fickle. They trade on being the first to know and share that with followers who look to them for that information. Unfortunately, you can't get too attached, because while they're promoting your product, they're also on the search for the next big thing. They'll love you and then they'll leave you. Their reputation depends on it. It's okay. Don't be too heartbroken, because if they do their job right, they'll help usher in the next wave of customers: your true-blue loyalists.

Though, in the end, we were able to do the impossible. We converted many of these love-'em-and-leave-'em trendsetters because we proved our value early and never wavered in quality of product or customer experience. Even the people who didn't care about cupcakes—only about knowing what's new and hot—referred us to people who did care about having a solution for delicious celebratory treats. We were a hot new find, but we also weren't going anywhere, because we provided the best solution out there.

COME OUT OF THE KITCHEN AND GREET YOUR CUSTOMERS

At the onset, it seemed like the entirety of Hollywood inadvertently became the face of Sprinkles Cupcakes. Without any soliciting at all, we found ourselves with several high-profile celebrity spokespeople: from Blake Lively expressing her love for Sprinkles Cupcakes on a national morning show to Ellen celebrating with vegan red velvets on her talk show, Pamela Anderson dropping a mention on *Jimmy Kimmel Live!*, Russell Crowe gushing on *The Tonight Show with Jay Leno*, Britney Spears, Selena Gomez . . . the list goes on. But when the hype calmed down and the business became more established, the next phase of our brand needed a fresh new face—which was apparently me.

We approached the branding at Sprinkles with great intention, but despite all of our precise planning, we didn't foresee how I would become such a critical core of the brand. In the early days of the business, when I was also employee #1, it was natural for me to connect with my customers, sharing my story of leaving the corporate world to pursue my passion. People didn't just start coming in for an afternoon treat, they stopped by to visit me. Some of our customers even started calling me Ms. Sprinkles (Charles, of course, was Mr. Sprinkles). The press was naturally drawn to my story, too, quickly labeling my journey "from banking to baking." Quite by accident, I came to personify the Sprinkles brand.

I could have named Sprinkles "Candace's Cupcakes," but I didn't. That was an intentional choice I made to ensure the product would always come first. What *Sprinkles* said was that this company is all about the cupcakes. But people still buy people, and I eventually realized that by stepping up and into my role as founder and face, I was giving people even more reasons to love, trust, and buy Sprinkles. It took me a minute, though, to get behind this new role. Hospitality is all about service and giving. There was something that didn't feel right to me about stepping out from behind the counter where I lovingly baked and boxed my customers' goodies.

I had always operated as the quiet one in the back of the bakery, making sure everyone had what they needed. I initially shied away from this more public role because this business wasn't about me—it was about the product and the customers. And yet, it was about me too. When you are proud of your product, people want to see that in you. I remember one customer buying a box of Sprinkles and telling me he planned to taste-test my product against a group of others from bakeries around LA. He asked me how I felt my cupcakes would stack up. I humbly replied that I hope he enjoyed them. I could tell he was disappointed. Did I not believe in my product, he wanted to know? To the contrary, I *really* did but didn't feel right boasting. I quickly learned that when speaking about my product, that was not the time for modesty.

It turns out that shouting from the rooftops that your product is the best helps customers feel good about the choice they are making. It's not some shallow ego trip, but about becoming a passionate advocate for what you do.

STEP INTO THE SWEET SPOTLIGHT

The first time I was called upon to be a spokesperson for Sprinkles on a national level was for a segment on a television news program called *Nightline*. I'd never really been front and center on TV before, and if I could write the script of my life, this was maybe the last moment I would insert a big media opportunity. I was still working long hours in the kitchen, in addition to navigating being a first-time mom with an infant. I had no clothes that fit and hadn't been properly introduced to the world of "glam" (hair and makeup). I was, as they said in the early aughts, the definition of a "hot mess." I'm sure most people saw a hardworking new mom who was somehow also juggling a category-defining business. But still, it was my first time realizing that I was inherently a representative of the brand, and I needed to start acting and looking like it.

It wasn't long after my debut that I received a call from a production company in Los Angeles. They were working on a show for the Food Network about cupcakes. The title of the show? *Cupcake Wars!* The owner of the company had been struck by the idea as she drove down little Santa Monica Boulevard, the location of our original flagship. She passed our store, and then a block later she passed another cupcake store (one from New York that had recently opened a block away to capitalize on the cupcake fervor we had inspired). She muttered under her breath, "It's a g**d*** cupcake war out there!" And, sure enough, she had the name for her show. The production company had decided on a competition show format and they needed the "queen of cupcakes" as their judge. Not knowing what to expect but understanding that I had to keep stepping into my personal brand power, I said yes. The original pilot was filmed under a tent on the UCLA campus and could have easily passed for a film school production.

It was a humble beginning, but the show struck a chord and became a hit on the Food Network, ultimately syndicating to other Food Networks around the world. I filmed more than one hundred episodes, next to my beloved French macaron master, Florian Bellanger, and my incredibly talented and magical friend Justin Willman. On every episode, I was positioned as the preeminent expert on cupcakes, and I presided at the judges' table, tasting, reviewing, and voting for my favorite cupcake. With each new season, our production studios improved, the sets became more elaborate, and the guest judges became increasingly famous.

I was on a hit show! I started getting autograph requests, being recognized at the grocery store and fielding offers to walk red carpets. All this translated into a halo effect for Sprinkles, positioning our company as the unequivocal leader in the field. What was most interesting to me was that the show encapsulated in a fun way what was truly going on in the national economy. In the aftermath of the 2008 financial downturn, many people had lost their jobs and were turning to entrepreneurship—and specifically cupcake bakeries—to make a living. With the job market offering little opportunity and the investment to start a cupcake bakery being relatively affordable, many saw starting a cupcake bakery as an attractive option. After all, America was mad for cupcakes! To think: just a few years earlier my cupcake idea was considered crazy; now cupcake bakeries were popping up everywhere. Many of these new business owners naturally wanted a turn at the title of *Cupcake Wars* champion, which they would then take home to their community and use as bragging rights to market their nascent business.

Stepping into my personal brand in the TV arena has ultimately built my reputation as a TV personality in and of itself. Though the early days were excruciating for me—a segment on the *Martha Stewart Show* left me sleepless and strung out with nerves for two weeks before and another national segment left me so anxiety ridden that I had a back spasm right before filming (the producer found me laid out on the green room floor)—I am relieved to report that I can now do any TV segment that comes my way without incident. I have *MasterChef, MasterChef Junior, Top Chef Junior, Good Morning America, The Today Show*, and many more under my belt, and it has led to new show opportunities like my role as a judge and executive producer on Netflix's *Sugar Rush*. Never in a million years would I have imagined that my decision to go to pastry school would lead to a career in Hollywood. But that is the true magic of entrepreneurship. Make one opportunity for yourself, and you'll find ten more waiting for you.

HOW TO BUILD A PERSONAL BRAND FROM SCRATCH

Whether or not you're planning on being the official face of your brand, you will be called to the forefront at one point or another, and it's important to be prepared. And, whether you're the spokesperson or not, building your personal brand, expertise, and thought leadership in your industry will only bolster your business. Here are the biggest tips I've learned firsthand:

Be comfortable with being a face.

It doesn't matter if you're selling baked goods, software, services, or even just your resume for a job interview—you must be comfortable selling yourself, and not just what you're offering. Ultimately, people are buying you, and not your product, and sometimes that can help give you the confidence you need to step into the spotlight.

Strong looks get noticed.

As I was initially thrust into the spotlight as the face of our company, I realized I needed to look as good as my cupcakes. The adage is true. You must dress the part. In the scrappy start-up phase, it was merely about survival. I was lucky if I had a moment to powder my nose with something other than sugar. Not that I needed to completely change my style, but I sensed that people might be expecting more from me at that point than the look of a harried baker who had stepped out from the back of the bakery in between batches. I didn't have to go full Hollywood—I just needed to present a more polished, camera-ready version of me. Sprinkles Cupcakes were fresh and pretty, and it made sense for me to present the same way, but how you present can mean something completely different for you. The key is that you are unapologetically yourself. If your whole vibe is nerd culture, don't try to go glam just for the camera. You have to be you—but make it the best and truest version of the persona you're trying to present.

Drive a stake in the ground.

When representing your company, reflect its brand values. Being the face of a family-friendly brand like Sprinkles means no racy Instagram posts or obscenities on podcasts, among other things. Luckily, the company I created and the brand extensions I was a participant in have always been a direct reflection of the values I possess. For me, living the responsibility to the Sprinkles brand is a piece of cake because these are the values I hold dear every day. Whatever your values, be true to them—not just when you're on the clock or within a certain medium, but consistently, across time and space. Show those values on social media and live them in your everyday interactions. True values are fixed. Be intentional with the way you present yourself and represent your brand. The bottom line is, just be a real person. Present the best version of yourself. Stay true to your core beliefs and, most important, lean into being front and center.

You don't need to be everywhere to get noticed.
With so many different media channels available, it can feel like there's pressure to have a robust presence on every platform. Don't fall for it! The more places you decide to present yourself, the more work you're creating to keep up, and the more diminishing returns you see. For instance, I hosted a podcast, *Live to Eat*, for a while because that space was booming, and I felt compelled to carve out my own corner where everyone was hanging out. But it just wasn't for me. While I love listening to podcasts, my heart wasn't into making one, so I let it go to focus on channels that suited my brand and personality.

Instagram has always been the platform of choice for Sprinkles because it lends itself well to a visual medium like cupcakes. Not every platform is right for your personal brand, which is an extension of your real self. As a thought leader in the entrepreneurship space, for example, I prefer LinkedIn or Twitter, but when I put on my pastry chef hat, Instagram is the most logical locale. There are plenty of social channels and outlets that do make sense for your brand, and that's where you should put your efforts and talent, because you have the best chance of maintaining a consistent presence that you enjoy participating in. There are plenty of social channels and outlets that could make sense for your brand. But, when it comes to a social presence, depth is more effective than breadth. Stick to a few channels with audiences and formats that resonate the most because it's there that you'll find the best chance of maintaining consistency, enjoyment, and authenticity.

FOOD FOR THOUGHT

It is increasingly common for founders to be the public face of their product. Ask yourself these questions to know if you're prepared to step into your spotlight:

Are you comfortable in front of a camera? You don't have to be ready for primetime TV, but can you turn your phone on yourself and speak to your audience via social media?

Do you know which medium is the best fit for your brand? Think about where your customers spend time online and what platform most naturally lends itself to your product or service.

Can you consistently conduct yourself in a way that authentically aligns with your brand's values?

Part Three
BUILD IT!

Channel Your Multitasking Operator

A s I sat down to explain the functions of operations, I kept coming up short. Not that I couldn't think of numerous job functions and roles. Quite the opposite—I was so overwhelmed by the litany of duties an operations person is charged with that I couldn't seem to sum it up! The responsibilities of any operations leader vary wildly depending on the industry or a company's phase of growth.

At Sprinkles, for example, day-to-day operations for one storefront meant ensuring equipment was working, ingredients were ordered, and the schedule was staffed. As we grew, it evolved to implementing systems, building and scaling units, and overseeing inventory management across the country. That same person was also the one dashing out to buy a generator to make sure someone's wedding cupcakes could be baked during a power outage (yes, this happened). It's a logistics-intensive position, and since logistics touches every part of the business, a good operator has to be nimble.

Founders may dream up a big, bold vision for their company, but it's how that vision gets carried out daily that determines its fate. That's why operators are charged with delivering on the strategy of the founder, *whatever* that may entail. It's a broad mandate, and a critical one. An effective operator is like grease on a squeaky wheel—an operational problem solver who makes things happen and optimizes the running of your business. The operations team ensures that the business is working every day, the product is getting into customers' hands consistently, employees are productive and paid, and there's a roof over everyone's head (or at least Zoom and a working Wi-Fi connection).

As a small business scales, it can often encompass HR, people management, team building, and even how the business gets funded and stays financially stable. Every start-up needs money to launch and make it to profitability. Whether you finance your new venture with funds from friends and family, a professional investor, or a surprise inheritance, you will need to dive into the finances as well. Being undercapitalized can deprive a company's growth of oxygen. Conversely, adding the right amount of money to a greedy business can be just the spark to supercharge it. So make sure you raise enough and manage that money so it can get you where you need to be—whether that's cash flow positive or your next round of financing.

See? It's a lot. And I barely scratched the surface. So, let's dive into what it takes to build that business once your big idea is off the ground.

Step Thirteen
PRICE OUT THE MENU

Know your worth and determine a revenue model.

I used to love talking shop with my hair stylist, Tyler. Though we peddled in very different industries, Tyler and I both had an entrepreneurial streak. Tyler wasn't just a business owner, he was a side-hustle king, and we loved to talk about how we were both planning to change the world with our innovative ideas. I remember one haircut appointment, right about the time I was super antsy to open Sprinkles. I was in a bit of a limbo after I had closed my home-based operations and while the space was under construction. All I could talk about was getting the store open.

While I was excited to bring Sprinkles to my small and devoted customer base, I knew I had to make some changes. First and foremost would be the price: It would have to increase with the additional overhead of running a retail store: rent, utilities, and employees. As I sat in front of the salon chair mirror, I figured I would ask Tyler, my trusted fellow entrepreneur, what he thought I should charge for a Sprinkles Cupcake. I watched him mull it over for a hot Los Angeles second.

He casually replied, "Mmm, 75 cents."

Seventy . . . five . . . cents?

"*What?*" I said, in disbelief.

"Well, you know . . . they're like donuts, and donuts cost about that much," he explained matter-of-factly.

Oh boy, I realized I had a *lot* of education to provide. Krispy Kreme we were not.

Fast-forward several months to me standing behind the Sprinkles counter every day, smiling despite the often-stomach-churning, sticker-shocked reactions from customers. I absolutely understood their confusion. At face value, forking over $3 for a cupcake seemed outrageous. Why would someone pay these prices when they could get a cupcake at the grocery store for less than a buck? Still, I justified my price until I was blue in the face. There was real *value* in my cupcakes: The quality of the ingredients, the process, and the care all supported the price tag. If customers remained unconvinced, I'd let it go, shrug, and say, "Just try one. You be the judge of whether this cupcake is worth $3." I almost always saw them again, but it was usually as they were walking out the door with a half dozen of them.

Our spot in Beverly Hills spoke to the inherent value of the product we were selling. We were a luxury boutique of sorts. Don't think of cupcakes as a luxury product? Well, step through our doors and you'll understand.

But it wasn't that easy. No one had ever thought of a cupcake as a premium product before, and there was a learning curve we needed to surpass. We were elevating the cupcake and using the best ingredients, so our price had to reflect that. Still, we got a lot of pushback. People had been conditioned to believe that cupcakes weren't supposed to be that expensive. We knew we had to turn this thinking around, so we worked tirelessly at every opportunity to educate our customers on our value proposition. While most skeptics could be turned around with a simple trial, we certainly didn't convince everyone. And that's okay, because you can't be everything to all people. As much as you want to convert everyone into a customer, you can't create a superior product at a budget price, which means you just have to let some people go.

PRICE YOUR BAKE SALE APPROPRIATELY

The shock of the price bought us literal time and an opportunity to explain what we were all about. Once I had their attention, it wasn't hard to enlighten people on the difference between a Sprinkles Cupcake and the crummy ones they were accustomed to buying from the supermarket. More important, I delivered on what I promised. Once they had a taste of Sprinkles, they were convinced—and they came back for more. For a segment of our customer base, the high price tag even became a selling point, signaling an implied value. "Wow, a $3 cupcake! It really must be something special." Over time, the price and value began to normalize in our community. After all, the price wasn't any more expensive than a tall latte from the local Starbucks, and there was so much more that went into it! It was a truly artisanal product, crafted from scratch daily.

The Beverly Hills location turned out to be a good move on many levels. Every tourist who comes to town wants the Rodeo Drive experience, but when we looked at the people walking the famed street, we didn't see many shopping bags. A simple T-shirt from one of its luxury boutiques can cost hundreds of dollars, and a handbag can run several thousand, so most people can't afford to purchase anything on Rodeo Drive. We found a way to fill that void and create equity in the neighborhood, allowing almost everyone who came to Beverly Hills to leave with a piece of that aspirational lifestyle. Soon, Sprinkles became a way for people to have that Rodeo Drive experience for less than $4.

When it comes to pricing your own product, look at your peers and competitors. Are you in line with them? If not, make sure your pricing passes the sanity check. Yes, Sprinkles was priced well above the current cupcake landscape, but we were doing something completely new, and we were backing up that price with an insane amount of value. I would argue that comparing a Sprinkles Cupcake to what was on the market at the time wasn't relevant because the two weren't comparable. Traditional cupcakes just weren't in the same league as Sprinkles when it came to quality, taste, craftsmanship, and presentation.

Even though our pricing surprised some people, it passed our sanity test because Howard Schultz had paved the way. Every day people from all walks of life were standing in line at their local Starbucks to pay $5 for a coffee drink without blinking an eye. Something that people used to exclusively brew at home or pick up at the gas station or Dunkin' Donuts was now fetching between $3 and $7 a pop . . . every day! Howard Schultz had done it with coffee, and we could do it with cupcakes. On a macro level, people were starting to care more about what they consumed, and they were showing up to pay for that quality.

What Howard did for coffee, I did for cupcakes. Sprinkles raised the bar in both quality and price. Competing copycat bakeries around the country were happy to piggyback on the education we spent time and energy cultivating, in addition to matching our normalized price point. However, their quality did not always rise to the occasion.

PEP TALK FROM THE KITCHEN

It's common for first-time entrepreneurs to undersell themselves and their product. It's hard to believe that anyone would pay for your idea, let alone that you could make a profit. And it's understandable that you'd want to make the barrier to entry as low as possible in the beginning. But I've seen it too many times—especially in female founders.

You're not doing anyone any favors by not charging what you're worth. Remember that you're providing a valuable service or product. Most important, you have to believe it. I could stand behind that counter all day talking about why my cupcakes were worth their price because I believed and knew it to be true.

Know how to properly value yourself and remember that a cheap price does not equal loyalty. Customers who are always looking for the best deal are typically fickle and will leave you once they find something cheaper. It's about creating that brand value. The only way to defend your price tag is to believe it yourself. If you don't believe your product is worth the price, how will anyone else?

HOW WILL YOUR BAKE SALE MAKE MONEY?

One of the most important things you'll decide in building your business plan is a revenue model. In other words, how is your company going to make money? Of course, it doesn't need to be just one way. Plenty of businesses operate with multiple revenue streams, but you do need to determine your *main* revenue stream. For instance, with Sprinkles, we sold a packaged cupcake mix through Williams Sonoma stores and created a Sprinklesmobile that we rented out for events, but our bread and butter (so to speak) was selling our cupcakes through our company-owned-and-operated retail outlets. This revenue model was ideal for us because we had control over the freshness and quality of our product and ownership over the hiring and training of our staff, which allowed us to have the most impact on customer experience. Owning the entire process from product creation to customer sale also allowed us to retain our entire profit margin. We could have pursued a wholesale revenue model—selling our cupcakes at a discounted "wholesale" price (usually 50 percent of retail) to other retail venues, such as cafes and restaurants, to resell them, but I never felt comfortable entrusting the Sprinkles experience to someone else. Not to mention, selling wholesale would have required a lot more volume to make up for the margin we would be giving away by selling wholesale, and I didn't want to become a manufacturing company.

We were approached by plenty of businesses eager to add Sprinkles to their menu of offerings, and none of them could understand how we could turn down an opportunity to get our product in front of more people.

After declining a wholesale request from a cafe in Beverly Hills several times, we were surprised to hear from one of our customers that our cupcakes were indeed being sold at their establishment. In fact, we didn't totally believe it, until we paid them a visit on our lunch break that day. Sure enough, front and center in the bakery case was a platter of Sprinkles Cupcakes, proudly marketed with homemade signage, FAMOUS SPRINKLES CUPCAKES. The cafe owners had been so desperate to sell our cupcakes that they were buying them at retail from our bakery, and then using them to lure customers into their cafe. We were shocked and fortunately they were cowed into removing them. Selling someone's product without their permission is one revenue model that I don't recommend.

Another revenue model we eschewed was the franchise model. Yes, people around the world were clamoring to open their own Sprinkles store, but we held steadfast to our original vision. Under a franchise model, aspiring business owners or "franchisees" could buy the right to own and operate their own Sprinkles bakery by paying a fee, or license, in addition to a percentage of the profits going forward. In return, Sprinkles would provide the right to use the name, recipes, proprietary ingredients, training, business systems, and marketing. As a franchisor you receive just a percentage of the revenue from each franchise, but the upside is that it offers the ability to scale quickly, accumulating that royalty over a larger number of units. Nothing Bundt Cakes is one business that went the franchise route and now boasts 410 franchises and counting!

While retail, wholesale, and franchises are well-established models, the internet has spawned myriad new trends and options that weren't even a thing when we started Sprinkles. Take the rise of peer-to-peer platforms, in which an online marketplace connects buyers and sellers who wish to exchange goods and services. Airbnb, an online marketplace for lodging, is one of the most successful to date, with more than 150 million users and more than 7 million listings in over two hundred countries. Airbnb profits with every transaction by charging a fee on both sides of the booking—to both the host and the guest. In return, they offer a trusted platform for easy communication, customer service, and payment processing. Other popular marketplaces include Etsy, where makers connect with buyers to sell their unique goods, and Uber's rideshare marketplace that connects drivers with those looking for transportation.

And who could miss the rise of digitally native vertical brands (DNVB)? These direct-to-consumer (DTC) companies, which started popping up around 2007, were web-only and broke from traditional retail models by manufacturing and selling their own products directly to consumers on-line. This DTC model cut out the middleman, passing along savings and offering full transparency to the customer. You may not recognize these acronyms, but you certainly know the brands that follow the model. Early DTC company and now e-commerce giant Warby Parker disrupted the way consumers shopped for eyewear and grew quickly—going public at a $4.5 billion valuation in 2021. Other prominent DNVBs, like mattress company Casper and sustainable footwear brand Allbirds, shook up their respective industries and followed similar trajectories to success, growing speedily by acquiring customers through digital advertising. But as the DTC market has grown increasingly crowded, advertising rates have increased, making it more expensive to acquire new customers and causing some of these players to make a return to brick and mortar.

Many direct-to-consumer companies have also embraced the sub-scription revenue model in recent years. Major household names like Blue Apron, Dollar Shave Club, and Stitch Fix were early pioneers that brought subscription-based products and services into the mainstream. For businesses like Sprinkles, based on one-off transactions, we were constantly sweating our next sale. But through a subscription business, revenue recurs automatically, giving visibility into future earnings and an established revenue base to build upon. This allows for freedom to focus on growth versus just making the rent. Investors are often enamored with the revenue predictability of a subscription model, and consumers enjoy the ease of having their products delivered and services renewed without having to actively manage them. You probably have a variety of fitness, entertainment, and productivity subscriptions—many of which go unused and unnoticed for far too long. No judgment! I'm right there with you. But it's a win for the business that gets to keep collecting revenue until you go out of your way to opt out.

For many technology apps, the revenue model is more of an afterthought, the foremost focus being on raising capital and acquiring users, figuring out how to monetize them later. Once an app has amassed enough users, they don't even have to charge for their product and can begin monetizing via advertising instead. If you have a Facebook or Instagram account, you know what I'm talking about. Anyone can download those apps for free but will inevitably be subject to a slew of "sponsored" ads in return. Of course, Facebook is the largest social network in the world, so all those eyeballs amount to a lot of advertising dollars! In 2020 it was a staggering $84 billion.

Not all apps follow the free model. In fact, the founder of the popular Facetune app, Zeev Farbman, bucked the prevailing tech trend and pursued an OG revenue model—one that's close to my heart—which he calls "the bakery model." He describes it like this: "You make a bagel, sell the bagel, buy ingredients to make more bagels, sell those bagels and on and on you go." Sound familiar? Just replace *bagel* with *cupcake*!

Unlike most of the apps on the market, which are free and often inconsistent in quality, Facetune perfected their product, then started charging for it right off the bat. It was a uniquely old-school strategy in a market dominated by free apps, but one that proved that it's a classic for a reason. On the heels of Facetune's success, its parent company, Lightricks, has since developed a suite of tools for photo and video editing and now boasts 5 million paid users across their offerings and a valuation of $1.8 billion. Facetune has certainly proven that the bakery model isn't just for bakeries anymore.

These examples are by no means a comprehensive representation of the many revenue models out there. Even in the app space between paid and free, "freemium" exists, which allows for the free download of an app, with some premium features hidden behind a paywall. Other revenue models include in-app purchases and affiliate sales. The list goes on—truly.

Before launching your business, make sure your revenue model is set and solid. As with any aspect of the business, check the competitive landscape to see how others are structuring their revenue and pricing their products. It will provide a good baseline for you to decide where to go, based on your own product or service.

FOOD FOR THOUGHT

There's no escaping the numbers when it comes to building a business. Make sure you have the answers to these fundamental questions before you launch:

How are you pricing your product or service? Is your pricing in line with the competition?

If you're higher, how do you plan to get customers on board?

If it's lower, why? Are you undercharging for the value you are delivering?

What is your revenue model (that is, how will your business make money)?

STOCK YOUR PANTRY

Streamline your operations and prepare to scale.

The first Sprinkles location took longer to open than anticipated, which left Charles and me plenty of time to really get prepped. So, naturally, we went to Vegas!

Okay, it wasn't an all-you-can-eat-buffet, blackjack-playing kind of trip. We were traveling to a major bakery expo in Las Vegas. We had the luxury of time, and we were all-in when it came to making sure we did our homework before launch.

Maybe it was seeing the Vegas strip lit up from the plane, or the naive optimism of being a first-time entrepreneur, but I arrived with some major stars in my eyes. I was about to launch a real bakery, and I was so excited to meet my colleagues—my people!

Charles and I had been to plenty of dull conventions in our past careers, but we had a feeling this would be different. We imagined it would be a charming walk past freshly baked goods, and we couldn't wait to don our name tags sporting the name of our newly registered business Sprinkles and start spreading the word. So, you can imagine my shock and disappointment as I passed booth after booth promoting the latest additives for extending shelf life and improving profits. My excitement at discovering a pile of glazed donuts was quickly dampened by the sales pitch that accompanied it—these "thaw and sell" donuts taste just like fresh baked! And they were drawing big crowds, as were the bake-off, freezer-to-oven, and dry mix offerings. So much for my charming bakery conference—this was more of a chemical convention!

We walked the aisles of the conference with our Sprinkles nametags talking about baking from scratch every day—and the industry vets laughed us out of the booths. "That's not the way to survive in the baking industry," they told us. There were moments when we wondered if this was just one big, expensive, self-indulgent journey. If enough people tell you you're crazy and you're going to fail, it starts to rub off on you. Was the universe trying to tell us something? Was this Viking Cooking School experience #2? We questioned ourselves. Why had we left high-paying jobs to take such a scary risk? Were we being delusional?

Let me be clear, there is nothing wrong with anything that was happening at the expo. Many hotels, supermarkets, restaurants, and cafes lack the time, money, and resources to make a wide range of baked goods in-house every single day. They rely on the modern, time-saving conveniences that were on display, such as dry mixes and thaw-and-sell frozen products. But these products weren't speaking to me or the bake-from-scratch business I envisioned.

Sure, the naysaying from the industry vets felt deflating, but after wallowing for a little too long, I began to see that this might be exactly the reason my mission was so vital. My approach flew in the face of every existing standard. I was building a first-of-its-kind product for the baking industry!

And it wasn't just the ingredients. We were also there to explore equipment. We looked at top-of-the-line commercial ovens—even though we had been warned not to buy new (only "rookies" bought new, while the pros bought refurbished ones). We also tested point-of-sale

(POS) systems—hardware and software systems that process transactions and keep track of sales, as well as other important data such as inventory. When we walked up to talk to the salespeople about what we were looking for, they were dismissive of our tiny operation, suggesting all we really needed was a cash register. I may have exuded confidence (after all, I had been one of only a few women at an investment bank—I knew how to fake a swagger), but inside I was wilting. I wasn't playing poker, but it definitely felt like I was the sucker at the table.

After a great dinner at one of Vegas's over-the-top restaurants, and a long laugh at how different our lives were since the days of tech conferences, Charles and I resolved ourselves. We would not be deterred. They could sneer at us all they wanted, but we believed in our dream. What if our oven broke down in the middle of the holiday season? New equipment came with a warranty and service—which we desperately needed—and we were more than willing to be the fools who paid the extra money for it. Honestly, what could be more important for our nascent bakery than a working oven? We knew we had to be thrifty, but we couldn't be shortsighted. This is also why we invested in a top-of-the-line POS system instead of just a cash register: because we had faith that we wouldn't be one little cupcake shop for long. We understood the value of having that data and being able to analyze those numbers. We were investing in our technology as if we were already a big company, because that's what we aspired to be. These early investments were costly and hard to justify initially, but they paid off in the long run.

Years ago, I learned a piece of wisdom from a chef in NYC that always stuck with me:

When you open a restaurant, you think it's going to be about the food and the service and all of these things. But what you don't realize is that it all boils down to the HVAC.

And it's so true! It doesn't matter how good your food is; if it's 90 degrees and your air conditioning is on the fritz, no one is dining at your restaurant. Or, if your walk-in fridge goes out, you don't have any food to sell. Sometimes running your business on a day-to-day basis boils down to these unsexy operational matters. It's not just the restaurant industry—if you launch a product, and your website goes down or there are issues in the supply chain, you are out of luck. No matter what business you're in, you might not always get a second chance to prove how great your product is if the operations can't get it to the customer properly.

SCALE YOUR KITCHEN

I had masterminded the cupcakes in my home kitchen, using my countertop mixer and cheap oven. When we opened Sprinkles, I wanted to preserve as much of what I had done at home as possible, but I quickly learned that I would have to make changes.

Firstly, standard commercial bakery ovens are all convection—which means there is a strong fan inside the oven to circulate the air for an even bake. But I wasn't used to using a convection oven, so the fan was blowing my extra-delicate cupcakes sideways as they rose. This led to a time-consuming dance of spinning the trays multiple times throughout the bake cycle.

Then there was the issue of volume. My original recipe yield of two dozen cupcakes was disappearing in a single transaction. There were days with a line out the door where we would count the cupcakes and be forced to scribble a makeshift sign that said, limit one per customer. You can imagine the frustration of driving across town to try the hot new cupcake place, finding elusive parking in downtown Beverly Hills, just to be told that you can buy only one cupcake! I remember one woman who was so irate that she publicly berated us, yelling about how inept we were and how our business wouldn't be around for very long. She was right on the first point but fortunately not on the second.

I had to upgrade the mixers and scale my recipes *fast*. Unfortunately, they did not teach this in pastry school, and baking recipes don't scale uniformly. So . . . all that time I had invested in perfecting my original recipe felt wasted when I was sent back to the drawing board, as I attempted to scale it using a mix of mathematical baking formulas (thank you, former finance life!) and good old-fashioned trial and error.

Of course, baking in those large batches meant we needed a *lot* more ingredients. You know that super-satisfying feeling you get when you return from a big grocery trip, and get to gaze at your perfectly organized and fully stocked fridge for a few days? We got to hold on to that feeling for approximately five minutes. We couldn't keep fridges stocked for more than one day at a time. In fact, we had a food supplier delivering every day as we filled our fridge and proceeded to empty it within a twenty-four-hour period. This was a laborious daily task, but it worked— until it didn't. The only problem with this system is that our supplier didn't deliver on the weekends, and we didn't have enough fridge space to buy the amount of butter and buttermilk we needed to get through the weekend. Our best solution? As soon as we'd emptied the fridge making batter and frostings on Saturday, we would make a run to Smart & Final and fit everything we could in my car to get through the rest of the weekend. Eventually we had the buying power to get our weekend delivery, but at first it was rough.

Ask our earliest employees; they'll tell you those first months were exhilarating but overwhelming. We all had to learn on the job, and the job was intense. Charles handled hangry customers in the front while I frantically baked in the back. We rarely delivered the experience we intended, but luckily most people gave us a second chance. In retrospect, the fact that Sprinkles Cupcakes were in such high demand and short supply added to the buzz surrounding our new business. Though that happened to work in our favor, my advice is to do everything in your power to fulfill your customers' demand for your product. It's rare that you will get another opportunity to prove yourself.

Charles and I had met working in corporate finance, where the hours were beyond brutal. We would stay up until dawn crunching numbers and making pitch books. When we decided to go into business together, we knew if we could endure those arduous work circumstances working for someone else, then we could get through anything working for ourselves. But there were nights during the early days of Sprinkles that made those corporate finance days feel tame. It was just the two of us handling hiring, scheduling, going on emergency ingredient runs, delivering orders to film sets, and building a website. Sometimes Charles and

I rolled up aprons and used them as pillows just to get twenty minutes of sleep on the cold, concrete bakery floor before we had to crank up the ovens again for the next day.

Even on precious days when I was off the schedule, inevitably someone would call in sick and I was back on. Charles would call me and say, "Time to put on your browns," in reference to the chocolate-brown T-shirt and khaki pants "uniform" we wore at Sprinkles. I remember driving home after one exhausting day after another without an end in sight. I would play a mental game with myself where I envisioned my life several years in the future when I couldn't possibly still be in this much grueling pain. It gave me a momentary lift.

Things came to a head when we began receiving threatening calls from the various utility companies saying they were going to turn off our gas or water because we hadn't paid our bill. Back at home, our bills were stacked in piles, blanketing our office desk. Although we had the money to pay our bills, we lacked the systems or time to deal with them. We were a commercial success, but organizationally, we were one big mess! When you're putting out fires all day long, you reactively turn your hose on the fire that's raging right in front of you. One day at the bakery we received a red notice that our gas would be shut off at midnight that night! After closing and cleaning as fast as we could, Charles and I rushed to a minimart to pay our bill in cash before the gas was turned off. Immediately after, Charles and I went to an office supply store to buy accounting and payroll software. Slowly but surely we were determined to implement some order.

Even though the demand for more cupcakes kept coming, we couldn't work any harder. The output was far outpacing the input with a skeleton crew. We even asked friends to help on busy weekends with shifts behind the counter. Our aspiring actor and writer friends thought it was a hoot—boxing cupcakes for celebrities at a bustling bakery. But this is only because hiring employees was terrifying, and we put it off as long as possible. How could we trust "our baby" with someone we hired off Craigslist? We had a few core employees who had been with us since day one. They referred their friends, and together we started building out our team. As we hired and recruited employees from other restaurants and retail companies, they brought with them experience with systems and procedures. We began to formalize the way we hired, trained, and operated. This would ensure all new employees were properly trained and that everyone understood the why and how of working at Sprinkles. We created manuals for new-hire conduct and customer service. No more flying by the seat of our pants.

That also meant we had to get real about what was feasible in-house. We were busting at the seams as it was, and it became clear that making all the cupcake decorations was becoming a bottleneck. True, I had discontinued fully custom decorations, but we were still making our modern dot decorations as well as a limited, set menu of decorations customers could choose from for special orders. All day long, hungry customers waited for cupcakes as they were whisked out of the oven, only to have to wait longer while someone furiously mixed fondant to our color specifications and cut the designs. It was silly. Customers didn't care about the decoration in most cases, but these dots were important to our brand. This was not scalable. We ultimately found a co-packer (short for contract packager—a company that packages products for other clients) that agreed to manufacture our decorations. We started with a small company, but they have grown with the business, and we have become one of their most important accounts. Conversely, we couldn't have grown the business the way we did without being able to outsource this all-important element.

Scaling at this rate was also possible because of our early investment in technological infrastructure, which provided an important foundation for future growth. We became *the* gift to give for all the top agencies and studios, and yet every single delivery and takeout order was handwritten on a notepad. We made it work but knew this way of doing business wasn't sustainable and was going to choke growth. At the time, our website was three pages of basic information. We knew we had to leverage technology to take the burden off our very lean staff.

We eschewed simple, inexpensive off-the-shelf solutions, instead developing a custom website optimized for online ordering that elevated the customer experience, allowing for mix-and-match flavor and decoration orders that could be picked up or delivered on any future date. At the same time, we invested in a dedicated customer service staffer and installed an "order line" to answer questions and place orders for those who still had questions or wanted that personal touch.

Efficiency is the holy grail. How much output can you create with the resources (typically limited for any start-up) you have? There are ways to do this with your human labor—making sure roles are allocated properly, and cross training where possible—but oftentimes it is more economical and efficient to rely on technology to automate systems instead.

TAKEAWAYS: WHAT DID WE LEARN?

1. **Spend the money where it makes sense.** For us, it made sense to buy new equipment with a warranty, because we couldn't afford to take any chances on something used.
2. **Start small but be prepared to re-create at scale.** It's hard to predict demand with any new venture, so be prepared for possible production, inventory, and supply chain issues. Expect it, lean into it, and learn from it.
3. **Leverage technology or other outsourcing.** Look at your operations—what is requiring the most time and money? Can you automate it or improve systems? If you outsource it or invest in some new technology, will it pay for itself?

OUTSOURCING:
SEND YOUR GOODS TO ANOTHER KITCHEN

This is all great advice if you're creating your own product, but what if you're outsourcing all the production? There is an entire spectrum from doing everything yourself to letting someone else handle it. We got a taste of this when we created Sprinkles mixes to be sold exclusively at Williams Sonoma stores. We designed a container and label, and then we pinpointed a local co-packer to make the mixes who already had an established relationship with Williams Sonoma. We met with them, then sent our recipes (after they signed a nondisclosure agreement, naturally), and they sent us round after round of mixes that we baked up and tasted, making tasting notes and suggestions until they got it just right. They started production, and all our baking mixes shipped straight to Williams Sonoma. We never had to touch any of it, aside from the initial taste testing! But if you don't have someone like Williams Sonoma guiding you, I recommend the most tried-and-true method: asking your network and doing the research.

● ● ● ● ● ●

Kroma Wellness is a nutrition company I personally loved so much that I became an investor. Founder Lisa Odenweller created her celebrity-endorsed five-day cleanse and accompanying products by experimenting with ingredients in her kitchen. Talk about scale. She went from a home-kitchen operation to launching a business with an astonishing number of moving parts that have to come together in an intricate choreography. Kroma's five-day reset requires 150 superfood ingredients sourced from around the world to create thirty-six individual SKUs. Putting the SKUs together requires six co-packers who send products to one final fulfillment center, where they're packed in the most complex way possible.

Although Kroma began as a single adaptogen latte product, Lisa wanted to make a greater impact on people's health, so she ultimately expanded the product offering to create an entire wellness program. Changing habits and transforming people's health over the long term is what truly excited Lisa, so she created a five-day reset in spite of the mind-boggling execution involved. "I wouldn't suggest anyone launch with this many products, but it was necessary for the business model because those are all the SKUs in our cleanse," Odenweller explained. "I had no idea what I was doing. I had never raised capital or put together a business plan."

On paper, Odenweller was completely unqualified to start Kroma. But her success can be attributed to never focusing on the "how." She was fully committed to tapping into her network and asking questions as she went. In looking for co-packers, for example, Lisa took to her network—both people she knew and total strangers. "You can go on LinkedIn and ask anyone who has built a product if you can pick their brain." She was particularly talented at finding people in the industry who knew more than she did and who were able to connect dots or teach. Every new contact led her to more answers, and questions.

Because of the complexity of what she was creating with Kroma, most fulfillment companies wouldn't touch it. Ultimately Lisa partnered with one who was excited about her vision and the potential growth of the business. Lisa stresses how important your relationships are—with the supplier, co-packer, fulfillment company, and beyond. You may be working with a best-in-industry co-packer, but if your business is too small for them to care about you, their sterling reputation doesn't matter. Look for suppliers and partners who are genuinely excited about your business, because it's the only way you can invest in each other for the long haul.

LISA ODENWELLER'S SPRINKLES OF WISDOM

Though she deals in wellness, Lisa is basically a wonderfully accurate fortune cookie when it comes to business advice. So, when you're in need of a little inspiration, come back to this page and pick a mantra or two.

- "When you know in your heart that you have to bring your idea/business to life, no one can stop you."
- "Everyone can start in their kitchen."
- "Have fun experimenting and playing with ideas. Share with friends and family to get feedback. They are your best 'test kitchen' to learn and evolve your idea from."
- "Don't be shy. And always be curious. Ask for what you need. People really do want to help."
- "Do the homework and always strive to be the best. At the end of the day, your product has to be the top product out there."

- "Often, your first idea isn't your final idea. Be willing to listen, learn, and pivot as needed."
- "It's important to learn from your customer before you can outsource customer service."
- "Do the due diligence and research everything you can to learn. But also trust your intuition. At the end of the day, your intuition is always your best guide."
- "Find partners who are in it with you. You need people who understand and care about you and your business and who will show up through both the good and bad times."

FOOD FOR THOUGHT

Operations can be a heavy lift, both literally and figuratively. It's important to be realistic about what it takes to build a business. As you move into ops planning, consider these questions:

Is there a version of your business that has the ability to start small and scale up?

Do you have the budget to invest in technology or automation solutions?

Are you up for the challenge of learning and troubleshooting?

Step Fifteen

FIND YOUR
COEXECUTIVE CHEF

Even solopreneurs need a squad.

s I've mentioned before, Sprinkles wasn't the first time Charles
and I worked together in a professional capacity. During our previous lives in the world of investment banking, he and I worked at
the same technology investment banking group. A banking industry tale
as old as time: An analyst and a more senior associate fall in love. Okay,
so it was less the stuff of fairy tales and more like the contents of a corporate exposé—remember those two burnt-out coworkers forced to toil
over pitch books for deals until all hours of the night who had no idea
they would one day end up sleeping on the floor of a commercial kitchen
together? We didn't date while working together, but it was definitely
where we first got to know each other. Even though the hours were

brutal, the camaraderie with all my colleagues was always tight. Nothing will bring people together more than shared misery. Yet, with Charles, it was different.

While I was an investment banking analyst, I noticed things about Charles and his work style that weren't like the other bankers around me. For one, he knew all the names of the garage parking attendants. He also knew details about their families, what sports teams they liked, and more. When I was assigned to work on potential deals with him, his approach was always one of collaboration and teamwork. And, if he was in the trenches with all of us analysts, he always made the drudgery more fun with a sense of humor. And, at the end of an extraordinarily long day, that's what mattered.

One of my primary jobs as an analyst was preparing pitch decks. These were presentations created by the bank to secure investment banking business—to convince technology companies to include us as an underwriter in their initial public offering, or to present an acquisition target as an idea for a possible merger or acquisition. Pitch books included financial models, the market opportunity, and our bank's competitive advantage. Like much of our work, they were typically put together under a tight deadline, which meant working into the wee hours of the night. But, as tired as we might have been, the details counted. I lost hours of sleep preparing these pitch books, and hours more in fear that some error had escaped my multiple read-throughs. The VPs and managing directors rarely did more than vaguely flip through the book in advance of the meeting, with the assumption that all was correct.

I remember one pitch meeting when Charles was leading the presentation to a data storage company called Seagate. The analyst who had created the book had accidentally typed *Seagram's* instead of *Seagate* in the pitch. You know, as in *Seagram's Escapes* spiked coolers? Of course, this was back in the day when presentations were printed and bound. This egregious blunder lived in infamy . . . in print. There was no backspace button or quick edit to remedy this mistake. No one in the meeting noticed until they all flipped their pitchbook pages in unison, and there it was—totally unmissable. Quick on his feet, Charles was able to play it off with the tech executives by making a joke—something to the extent that maybe they could all use a drink—and not letting it derail an otherwise intense meeting. I know from being in the room for many pitches that if there had been another associate leading the meeting, the presentation might not have gone so smoothly.

I had no idea that it would be moments like the Seagate pitch that would assure me that going into business with my husband would be a strength. Having been happily married for over two decades, I can safely say we work well together, in life and in business. From the boardroom to the bakery, we've always been there to support one another, excitedly bouncing ideas back and forth. When I decided to start Sprinkles, we were both so convinced of the concept, he was willing to jump ship on a successful career in finance to help me sell cupcakes. His total belief in me was such a motivating propellant. It's easy to have an incredible idea and never let it grow to be anything other than a dream. But, when you have another person you trust who is not only encouraging you to follow that dream, but offering to help build it, you have to lean in.

THE CASE FOR A COEXECUTIVE CHEF

While I was sweating it out making my elaborate cakes, Charles had left the intense world of investment banking and moved into financial consulting. At one point, after I began toying with the radical idea of cupcakes as my next move, he told me that if I could master my recipes, he would join me in this crazy cupcake venture. Challenge accepted. It was just the push I needed. Knowing that I would have a partner in getting my business off the ground made it seem more possible. I doubled down on my recipes and started treating it less like a hobby and more like a job. He had played into my competitive side by challenging and inspiring me to perfect my product. And just like that, I had my cofounder!

You may have a great idea and believe you're ready to start your business by yourself. While going it alone is a totally viable option, let me offer a case for considering a cofounder. I've said it before, but I'll say it again: *Building a business is hard.* So hard that I believe it can sometimes be overwhelming if you try to go it alone. Finding a partner who shares your vision, complements your skill sets, and has your back is one of the most important things I believe you can do to set yourself up for success. In fact, many venture capital firms insist on a cofounder before investing. Harj Taggar, a partner at Y Combinator, a prestigious accelerator, believes that the *most* important part of starting a company is finding the right cofounder. He says a cofounder is essential for success because of the increased productivity and moral support you receive from a partner. Not to mention, many of the most successful companies in the world (ahem . . . Apple, Facebook, Google, Microsoft), although we now associate them with just the CEO, were cofounded.

IT TAKES TWO!

A udrey Wu, founder and COO of Ruth Health, a telehealth clinic for pregnancy, met her current cofounder, Alison, when they were speakers on a panel about artificial intelligence. The two clearly infused a technical topic with personality because the post-panel feedback was that they were the most engaging speakers there. Audrey and Alison immediately became friends and it wasn't long before they had cooked up a new business idea: Dioptra, a more comfortable speculum, won them two FDA grants before they ultimately pivoted to founding Ruth Health. Both Audrey and her cofounder Alison have "big and charismatic personalities" but have found balance in their respective roles— Audrey enjoys operations whereas Alison prefers a more public-facing role. Audrey says, "This is my third start-up and I feel it is critical to have a cofounder. Magic happens when you have the right founding team who provide diverse perspectives." Her advice to those looking for a cofounder? "Say *yes* to the panels, the conferences, and the networking events. You never know who you're going to meet!"

While you can and *should* build a strong team, develop a great network of people to support you, and even gather a stellar board of expert industry advisors no matter what, none of these people will likely want to hear from you in the middle of the night when your website goes down. A business partner or cofounder occupies that special and singular space of someone entirely aligned with your goals, willing to put in the extra-long hours and sacrifice. They push you, balance you, celebrate the wins with you, and pick you up off the floor when you don't think you can do it one more day.

It's kind of like . . . being married, which makes sense why so many life partners become business partners (ahem . . . Rita Wilson and Tom Hanks, Joanna and Chip Gaines, and Kelly Ripa and Mark Consuelos, just to name a few).

Ask my husband and me who came up with the idea for the Cupcake ATM, and we'll both say, "I did!" It's not that we're trying to take credit for something we didn't do (it was me), but the reality is that when you have a partner in your business who knows your business as intimately as you do, the lines start to blur. In a true brainstorm, people's ideas build on one another, and it's a safe space to recommend crazy or off-the-wall ideas. When you have a trusting relationship with your cofounder, you know they aren't going to mock those ideas; they'll even be inspired by them. In fact, this is exactly how brainstorming was supposed to happen. Alex Osborn, an advertising exec who coined the term *brainstorm* in the 1950s, advised: "Toss out as many ideas as possible. Don't worry if they're too crazy. Build on the ideas people generate. Don't criticize initially." If you've ever participated in a good brainstorm, you know that's when the breakthroughs happen.

The partnership between Charles and me was a key factor in the success of Sprinkles because we supported each other and allowed our complementary skill sets to shine. For instance, my strengths were in the creative, leading product creation, branding, marketing, PR, and customer experience. Charles was talented with logistics like real estate, finance, operations, and management. Could I have navigated the commercial real estate world? Sure. Would it have been the best use of my skills? Absolutely not. I was allowed to focus on the things I was passionate about and, frankly, good at.

Having a partner allowed me to divide and conquer, which became critical as Sprinkles grew at an astronomical rate. As our celebrity status grew in Hollywood, there were more demands on my time outside the kitchen as a brand ambassador and spokesperson from media to TV shows. This meant long and unpredictable hours spent representing Sprinkles on the small screen. While I preferred to be behind the counter, these media opportunities were vital for brand exposure. I would never have felt comfortable leaving my business for weeks on end while I filmed *Cupcake Wars* if Charles wasn't in the bakery making sure things were running to our standard. I'll admit it here, in print, he even became a pro at baking and frosting cupcakes.

Of course, most of my friends couldn't imagine working with their spouse. Trust me, I get it! This stuff is difficult, even for the hardest-working and most optimistic of us all. When your partner's business and life dreams align with yours, the perks are awesome, but proceed with caution because the stakes are high.

Starting a company is stressful and can be taxing on even the strongest of relationships. Resolving conflict is a huge part of any relationship, but it's extra critical when it comes to running a business. There will be times when you disagree with one another, so make sure you have a communication style that allows you to navigate those bumps in the road. Luckily Charles and I have found that humor—which has always played a huge role in our relationship—helps us traverse those tricky times.

HOT TIP

How you work through disagreements is just as important as how well you work together! Avoidance, anger, passivity, or being overly accommodating are all unhealthy styles of conflict resolution.

THE 3 CARDINAL RULES FOR COFOUNDING WITH YOUR SPOUSE

1. **Communication is key.** Schedule times to talk and check in during the workweek so you don't bring it home with you. In the early days of Sprinkles, Charles and I worked all day long next to each other in a small six-hundred-square-foot space, so we didn't feel like there was any need to set up meetings to connect, plan, and analyze what was working. Don't mistake working side-by-side with someone for working in sync with them.

2. **Set boundaries.** Too often (always) we brought work home with us. We had no clear boundaries between work and home life. When you own your own business and live with your partner, the work never stops, so you have to create boundaries. Set a time when the phones get shut off and you stop checking your computer. Have a conversation with your partner about something other than work. Rest your mind and nurture your relationship.

3. **Make sure you have roles clearly delineated at work and at home.** Sometimes the home stuff isn't as clearly defined— and it needs to be. If you both have an important meeting, and your child is sick, and someone needs to take him to the doctor, who's it going to be? Does one person own that responsibility or is it case by case? Either way is fine, if you discuss it in advance and everyone has buy-in. If one person feels like they are always the one sacrificing, there's going to be resentment.

CAN THERE BE TOO MANY COOKS IN THE KITCHEN?

Even though I stumbled upon my cofounder sitting next to me on the couch, that doesn't mean that's where you'll discover yours. You may not plan on being married to your business partner, but a functioning cofounder relationship relies on the same basic principles as a good marriage: trust, compatibility (it's okay if opposites attract!), collaboration, conflict resolution, and ultimately the ability to compromise.

The cofounder relationship can take on many forms: friends, family, acquaintances, or someone you don't even know yet. When you're on the hunt for a cofounder, look for someone who complements your skill set while also sharing the same drive and ambition. If it seems like you're looking for a unicorn, you are. And, sometimes, you might not find all these qualities in just one person.

Take La Ligne for example, an apparel company with three cofounders. Former *Vogue* editors Valerie Macaulay and Meredith Melling and Rag & Bone's former head of business development Molly Howard joined forces with one goal: translate the stripe into a collection that would empower women of all ages with effortless self-expression.

It wasn't always a trio. Valerie and Meredith had been colleagues at *Vogue* for ten years. As the bookings editor, Valerie had the casting office, overseeing models, while Meredith was a senior market editor and fashion director at Vogue.com. During that time, they shared many conversations about what constituted the "classic uniform." After *Vogue*, while the idea for La Ligne was percolating, they spent time consulting with fashion brands. Through their experience at *Vogue*, they had seen firsthand how hard it is to get a brand off the ground, so they wanted to get the lay of the land before launching their own.

When the pair finally started floating the idea of La Ligne by trusted business colleagues, everyone pushed back at the fact that they were two creatives. Who would run this company, they asked? Where was the CEO? They knew they needed someone to run the business but had always imagined this person would be a salaried employee, not another cofounder.

Valerie and Meredith knew of Molly's stellar business reputation in the fashion community. Molly had an extensive network in the industry, having been raised in a fashion family, working in finance at Credit Suisse and then at Rag & Bone. So they showed her their pitch and asked her if she could refer any CEOs their way. To their amazement, she came back to them with a full business plan and financial model projecting the future of La Ligne's direct-to-consumer model and just one request: to make her a cofounder. How could they say no to that? She was exactly what they needed to get La Ligne launched.

The decision to bring on a third partner was a leap of faith, but Molly had made a powerful first impression. With three smart women at the helm, they decided to divide and conquer, exercising power within their respective domains. While all three are cofounders, they hold different titles and lead separate areas of the business. Molly is CEO, Meredith is CBO (chief brand officer), and Valerie holds the title of CCO (chief creative officer). While threesomes often get a bad rap, with one always feeling left out, the La Ligne cofounders have found the opposite to be true.

"We all have these complementary traits," Meredith says. "I remember noticing this about Val at *Vogue*. She's so decisive. I always need to consider the twenty options, but Val has a great gut and it's always right."

"And I appreciate the camaraderie," Valerie explains. "If I have a problem, I text them both. I love having that collaboration, and not working inside a vacuum. Having these smart women in the room with you to help flesh out ideas."

One unique benefit of having three cofounders is that the trio decided that the majority always rules. Normally, they're all on the same page but, if not, it goes in the direction of the new majority. For them, it makes it so much easier to let go of a disagreement and move on.

Ultimately, no matter how many cofounders you have, it comes down to trust. "I completely and totally trust Meredith and Molly, whether it's a new store or campaign," affirms Valerie. "We're all talking about it, but inherently trusting that the other person has their space."

Meredith adds, "When we were first establishing the DNA of the brand, everyone needed to sign off, but once we solidified the founding language of the brand, we were able to move forward confidently in our own areas."

"And," Valerie says, "we have a lot of fun doing it."

EVEN A SOLO CHEF NEEDS A TEAM

While my experience was always with a partner, I've seen plenty of solo founders rise to success. But how do they do it? I asked Jesse Draper, founding partner of Halogen Ventures, an early-stage venture capital fund investing in female-founded consumer technologies.

"I believe that a solo founder can definitely be as successful as a co-founder. If you are a solo founder, you need to make sure that you have a team who can handle everything if you were to step away, have a baby, experience a major illness, or something else unforeseen at the time you raise money for your company. Building a company is a ten-year marathon, so things happen."

As an investor, Jesse typically asks solo founders questions like this: "Do you have someone on your team who you can lean on? A great COO? A killer CTO? Someone who can lead in your absence?" Typically, a healthy C-suite can handle this but, in the earliest stages of a company, you don't have a fully built-out C-suite, so you want to make sure that there is someone else on the team who can support you. For a venture capital investor, it's important that their investment is protected in every way possible, and usually that means more support—whether that's in the form of a cofounder or a trusted team to back up a founder. Whether you are a solo founder or a cofounder, you want to make sure that you are putting the business first and always acting in the best interest of your company and your investors and shareholders.

MAKE SURE EVERYONE GETS A PIECE OF THE PIE

One of the best ways to make sure you and your cofounder are aligned is by sharing in the equity. Some founders make the decision to do a fifty-fifty split, while others decide on the split later once the roles and responsibilities have crystallized. Either way, it's best to work with a good lawyer to set up your equity with a vesting schedule.

Vesting refers to how the equity you own in the company becomes available to you and is sometimes used as a mechanism to protect cofounders. If your cofounder leaves within the first few months and does nothing more for the company yet keeps 50 percent of the equity, it's not fair to the remaining cofounder who is now shouldering the burden alone. Vesting ensures that the people who are still there doing the work get the rewards of that sweat equity. Typically, equity vesting follows a three- to five-year schedule with an equal number of shares vesting at the end of each year. This means that if your cofounder drops out within the first year, they won't have any shares to show for it. Once they had been at the company a year, they would have 25 percent of their shares vested if they were using a four-year schedule. Also, many companies have a buyback right for shares when a founder or other equity holders leave.

FOOD FOR THOUGHT

No founder is an island, even when they're the only ones technically in charge. Before you choose your partners and confidants for the journey, consider these questions:

Is this person as excited about your idea as you?

Does this person have a complementary skill set to your own?

Do you feel it's possible to establish clear roles that play to each of your individual strengths?

Do you have a system for working through decision making and disagreements?

Do you have a contract that protects your company equity in the case that your cofounder leaves?

Step Sixteen

CONTINUOUSLY
WHISK IN CULTURE

Cultivate a people-first culture.

y first introduction to company culture was defined by a lack thereof. The fight-or-flight, sink-or-swim environment of an investment bank during an economic boom was solely about output and performance. My next experience, during the buzzy internet bubble of the late nineties, was decidedly different. Culture suddenly became an important new priority as internet companies scrambled to entice talent to take a risk on their new business. Casual dress, Yoga Mondays, Free Lunch Fridays, and break rooms stacked with ping-pong tables and snacks became the definition of corporate culture, which, in turn, became a literal perk.

It wasn't just inflated in-office experiences. I remember one over-the-top (literally) team building offsite that took place in Napa Valley. It included a hot-air balloon ride, skydiving (I politely waited on the ground), and dining at famous restaurants in the area. Was it fun, exciting, and a totally luxurious experience I never would have had otherwise? Yes. Was it necessary to connect with my coworkers and feel closer to my team? Absolutely not.

Superficial culture value props were a carrot that companies dangled as evidence of just how "fun" it was to work there. And, because culture was all about tangible items, and not what we now understand to be real employee benefits, it became a race to outcompete with the next shiny offering.

As I've become an employer myself, it's become very clear that company culture can't be distributed or scheduled into the workweek. Culture comes from living your company's core values and infusing those through your workplace. So how do you create this elusive, intangible thing that's felt more than seen? Initially, it happens very organically, flowing naturally from a founder who is interacting with their team every day. If your company values and mission are intact, and you're walking the walk, you're creating company culture without even trying! Of course, as your company gets larger, you will want to be more intentional about the way you approach company culture, to preserve as much of the magic of those first few years as possible. The goal is to establish a company culture that is so strong, it can survive even after you make an exit.

WHAT HAPPENS IN THE KITCHEN DOESN'T STAY IN THE KITCHEN

Your customers aren't the only ones moved by your company's mission and brand values—those things drive your employees too. A strong culture helps you keep your employees motivated and engaged by propelling them to give their best effort and become brand evangelists to both prospective customers and employees. Good culture doesn't just fuel your current team, it also helps attract new talent.

Think about what has motivated you and kept you happy at the various jobs of your past. I'd bet there was much more to it than the number of dollars on your paycheck. Though it's often treated like a transactional experience, a job has never really been such, and it's becoming less so. In my experience, millennials and Gen Zers increasingly choose a job based on the mission and values of the company; they want to be personally aligned with their work, and studies show that Gen Z is especially motivated by a strong company mission and culture.

At Sprinkles, our mission and values remained firmly intact: connection, nostalgia, and fun. This made it a truly joyful place that brought people together and allowed them to forget the frustrations of life outside. How did we create this down-to-earth utopia in the middle of a notoriously fake Hollywood scene? We delivered a winning combo of the most delicious product and the best customer service. You could feel the joy the moment you walked through the doors. Our Beverly Hills store had the energy of a great party, with a bustling bakery in back, a busy store packed with customers in front. Charles bounced around between the cupcake stand and the register, and I ran freshly baked cupcakes to and from the kitchen. The space was so small and cramped that our cupcake associates coined the term *the Sprinkles Dance* to describe the way we squeezed and whirled by each other trying not to step on toes or crush fragile cupcakes. It was electric!

Charles and I also brought a unique business mentality from our banking and tech days that felt much more like a start-up than a bakery or restaurant. We had a "do whatever it takes" mindset and empowered our team to be the same way. That meant we looked for employees who were enthusiastic and willing to problem solve. We found that this attitude was much more important than any previous bakery experience. We could train most people to do the work as long as they had that positivity and embodied our customer service philosophy.

Sure, we were in the food business, but it was all about hospitality. Ultimately, what I wanted to do when people walked through the door was take care of them. So in hiring, I also looked for those who took a genuine interest in people. For me, baking is truly about giving, so I sought out those who exhibited a similar generosity of spirit. I was obsessed with Sprinkles, and that passion infused the air—and every interview—with electricity, attracting people who were vibrating at that same frequency. For employees who fit our culture, and were able to master the skills, the sky was the limit. We began promoting, and ultimately moving, managers to different markets to lead stores or supervise regions.

HOT TIP

If you hire the right person, then managing them is, well, cake! So, I say, "Hire tough and manage easy."

When we did hire outside the company, we recruited from businesses we admired. But we were often disappointed when we recruited people from the hallowed halls of elite hospitality. We looked up to companies like Hillstone Restaurant Group (Houston's) and Starbucks and wanted to learn from people who had been trained and brought up in these organizations but found that it wasn't as easy as just bringing on their former team members. We were doing things our way, having brought best practices from a different industry, which meant there was often a cultural misfit with restaurant lifers. Though it was a learning curve, it was gratifying to realize that we had built our own culture and systems, organically—and it was working well. We had invented our own special sauce!

Company culture, when you really boil it down, is how you make people feel every day. It's about how you make your employees feel valued, inspired, and motivated. In my past job experiences this had never been much of a priority. Case in point, when one of the managing directors at our investment bank randomly chose an analyst (like me) to sit in the passenger seat just for carpool-lane privileges to drive to his meetings in Silicon Valley, the analyst would then have to recoup those lost hours by pulling an all-nighter at the office later that night. I'm pretty sure he never thought twice about whether we felt valued—and it showed. I was determined to do things differently than my own experience by empowering people. For instance, it was a major priority to give our cupcake associates the power to gift up to a dozen cupcakes to turn around a customer's dissatisfaction.

CULTURE WON'T JUST BAKE ITSELF

Once you've hired your dream team, company culture doesn't just magically coalesce. The right people are the main ingredients, but you still need someone to oversee the recipe. And, just like baking, you really must watch your cake in the oven. Turn your back for a moment too long, and it could burn.

Culture is made collectively, but it can't go anywhere without strong leadership directing it from the top. Trust me, everyone is watching you. Charles and I embraced the servant leader's way of doing things. In other words, nothing was beneath us. We led by example and did the work. When any new salesman came into the store, he would look around, notice Charles polishing some corner of the floor and me covered in flour, and assume the decision-maker was not present. He'd then hand off whatever he was selling to me and say, "Can you give this to the owner?" Now, if Charles and I had remained in the bakery for too long, we wouldn't have been able to grow and scale, so I'm not saying you should be sweeping the floors forever. It's more about modeling what's important. If cleanliness and details are important, be sure you aren't above doing the work and pitching in. Support your team. Come into your workspace and ask how you can help. If it's clear your team is in the weeds, jump in without asking.

Make sure to celebrate your team's accomplishments. Did someone receive an outstanding review on Yelp? Perhaps a customer specifically took the time to report an impactful experience with a team member. When your employees go above and beyond for you, it's your responsibility to repay the effort and honor. We created "Sprinkles service stars," which allowed managers to reward team members for great customer service. This not only incentivized our associates, but also led to more engagement by our managers who were actively observing and coaching their employees. It also led to friendly competition among staff because the team member who earned the most service stars was re-warded with a bonus for the month. We created a healthy, supportive environment that made hourly employees want to perform and, in turn, encouraged managers to be watching more intently.

And, unlike the tech start-ups in the late nineties, we understood that real work perks didn't involve a flowing beer tap. I'll bet we were the only small cupcake shop that offered a 401(k) for both hourly and salaried employees. Offering real benefits was one of the many reasons we were able to retain loyal talent. Especially in high-turnover industries like re-tail, restaurant, and hospitality, it's a big deal to reach a work anniver-sary. Loyalty is hard to come by in any business, and it should be acknowledged, respected, and publicly celebrated within the organiza-tion. We celebrated our employees' work anniversaries with certificates, then jackets, and then bonuses every year. It didn't matter if it was a general manager or dishwasher, everyone received the same level of appreciation.

While we were bonded together by our love of Sprinkles, we all brought a diverse range of talents into the bakery. Particularly in a place like Los Angeles, many of those who work in the food world are pursuing other dreams outside their hourly day job. We had an *American Idol* alum help behind the counter before landing a hit TV show, a delivery driver who was a screenwriter, and a manager who is now a celebrated inde-pendent film producer. Encouraging other priorities outside of work builds a more eclectic team, and it gives everyone the creative outlets they need to feel great when they walk into work. When people are given room to pursue what they love, they come to work as a more whole person, which contributes to a rich company culture and guest experience. We made it a point to not only hire bakers, frosters, and cashiers, but also actors, singers, surfers, and students.

EMPLOYEE SPOTLIGHT: MAUREEN BHAROOCHA

Lean into the talents your employees already possess. One of the team members at our Beverly Hills location wasn't just a great store manager, she was also a very talented film school graduate. Her dream was to be a director, and she felt that it would be impossible to achieve this goal if she stayed working at Sprinkles. We didn't want to hold her back, but we also didn't want to lose her.

So we gave her a small budget to create short films we could use as marketing spots for Sprinkles. (Keep in mind this was pre-Instagram reels!) Guess what? Maureen stayed for years after that, made some amazing commercials for us, and eventually went on to work as a segment director on *Jimmy Kimmel Live!* and, ultimately, lived her dream by making her own independent films.

She is in the press quite a bit now, and every time she's interviewed, she talks about her early days at Sprinkles. We had incredibly high-quality content being created by someone who intimately knew and loved our business like we did. We couldn't have hired outside the firm for that. And I'm so proud of her!

Sprinkles gave me a unique opportunity to bring myself (and my creativity) to my job. The valuable skills I learned at Sprinkles, I still use today as a director. Candace saw value in helping others make their dreams a reality. I'm proud to be part of the Sprinkles legacy.

—Maureen Bharoocha

MAINTAIN A MISSION-DRIVEN CULTURE

Sprinkles had a strong, clear mission and we grew extremely fast. To maintain the mission and build a culture around it in a quickly expanding business was not easy, and I admire anyone who is able to do it, such as Denise Woodard, founder of Partake Foods.

Denise's cookie company had a strong culture of inclusion from the get-go, stemming from the name alone. The concept of an allergen-free snack arose for Denise when her daughter was diagnosed with severe food allergies as an infant. Denise and her husband came up short on healthy snacks that were both delicious and safe to eat. So, frustrated by the lack of options, Denise left her corporate job and set out to make her own.

Though the product is geared toward inclusion for people with food allergies, the ethos of the business reaches higher. Partake aims to push for inclusion in business as well as the food system by addressing the issue of food scarcity. "Thirteen million kids don't know where their next meal is coming from," Denise says. Partake's mission wants to tackle not just food shortages, but also inequalities. Allergen-free food is often much more expensive, and food pantries often have extremely limited options and quantities of allergy-friendly foods.

So, how does Denise make sure she puts her mission where her money is? The company's team is 93 percent women and 60 percent people of color, they launched the Black Futures in Food & Beverage fellowship program, and Partake partners with a give-back program that has fed over five thousand families. With such a strong company mission, it was easy for Denise to allow it to lead the culture on her fast-growing team. Belief in the product and company's impact will innately build a motivated, dedicated, and like-minded team. But the day-to-day experience has to match the lofty, high-level goals in order for that energy to sustain.

The foundation of the company culture—feeling welcome, safe, and respected—comes from her product's inspiration, her seven-year-old. "It's how we treat our employees and everyone who comes into our office," Denise says matter-of-factly.

All of her employees were hired during the pandemic, which meant she had to grow the team remotely, eventually going back with a flexible work schedule. It was important for the culture to be reflective of Denise's own life. "We have lots of working moms on the team. If you need to work early, get the kids ready for school, and then hop back in, that works," explains Denise. She understands that the only way to grow her business and spread her mission is to have happy employees who are allowed to show up as their full, best selves.

Plus, every employee gets all the cookies they can eat. You can't really beat that . . . unless it's fresh cupcakes. Even then, that would be a hard call, even for me.

FOOD FOR THOUGHT

A business is only as strong as its weakest link, and a solid company culture is one of the best ways to make sure you're building a successful brand based on a happy and supported team. As you think through the environment you envision for your brand and its employees, consider these questions:

What are the qualities of an ideal employee?

What can you offer a potential candidate to help them feel valued?

If your goal is to be a people-led company, think about what that means to you. How will you put that into action?

Step Seventeen

KEEP THE OVEN LIGHTS ON

Find the right funding for your business.

When I went to college, my parents gave me a lovely sendoff complete with pride, well wishes, and a used Saab hatchback that would carry me through several careers and life moments. It served me tirelessly all through college, all through my years in San Francisco, and then helped us make the move to LA. At this point, it was starting to lose steam, but with the large investments we were making in our business, Charles and I couldn't afford a new car. Plus, the huge trunk was a godsend when it came to making deliveries and emergency trips for ingredients. The roof liner started to sag, so much so that it would touch the top of our heads as we drove around. We tried different homespun methods for keeping it up, including glue and duct tape, but no matter what, it would fall. We figured it was just cosmetic; the car still ran well . . . until it didn't. It started giving out.

At one point, it conked out on me in the middle of a busy intersection in West Hollywood and I was mortified. On the corner was a popular coffee shop and the outdoor tables were filled with people watching the world go by. All eyes turned to me in my car, blocking traffic in the middle of the street. A few wonderful souls sprung up from their iced blended coffees and helped me push it into the shoulder. It was really time for a new car, but we were merely months into Sprinkles and the business needed a stand mixer—a huge piece of machinery and major investment that would mean all the difference for our output at the bakery. So, what did we do? We took the car to the shop to get it cobbled together, and bought a brand-spanking-new stand mixer, which might as well have had leather seats and power steering for what it cost. Sure, I wouldn't be cruising the Pacific Coast Highway in it, but it would take me on a much more fulfilling ride.

DELAY GRATIFICATION

Choosing a commercial kitchen appliance over a much-needed new car was one of the many sacrifices I made while building my company from idea to empire. For us, bootstrapping felt like the only option because there was no bank on the planet that would have given a loan to two out-of-work investment bankers who wanted to bet it all on cupcakes. And venture capital was out of the question. We knew enough about the market to be realistic that bakeries were not known for high growth or big liquidity events. Fortunately, we were able to fund it ourselves.

We did this by postponing homeownership to use our savings for a business instead. Charles and I had been able to collectively save a decent amount in a few ways. One of the upsides of betting on working at a dot-com was having the ability to cash out. I had some stock options from my former job, and Charles had collected a fee for advising on the sale of a small internet company. Though we both did well in our respective careers, it's much easier to build a nest egg when you get a chunk or bonus like that, versus siphoning off part of your biweekly salary every week, and in that way, we were very fortunate. These weren't stratospheric exits, mind you, just enough to live on modestly for a couple of years while we patched our idea together. We used that money to develop the product, create the brand, and open our first location. We cut personal expenses and dug deep into our reserves, which we spent frugally but wisely, focusing on what was important at every step.

But what did bootstrapping really look like on a personal level? It meant we had to say goodbye to all the luxuries we had enjoyed while living on a nice salary. No vacations, no fancy dinners, and no new clothes. More than extravagances, it meant putting a pin in all nonessential expenditures—like all of them. Clearly the car was one, but so were my teeth, evidently. I remember one rather awkward and embarrassing exchange with an LA dentist who insisted on filling a cavity with porcelain. After I heard the price tag, I refused anything but silver; it would do just fine. He tried his best to convince me, invoking the pride I had in my own work as a parallel. He didn't want to be known for a mouth with silver fillings just as I wouldn't want to be known for a poorly made cupcake. While I appreciated the commitment to the integrity in his work, honestly, I wasn't having it. Money was tight and disappearing quickly as that perfect first location kept eluding us for months longer than we had planned. I held firm and offered to go elsewhere for the work. I ultimately got my silver filling, but not without a fight. Every dollar was precious, and whatever we could scrimp on we did, to preserve cash for our business. I still have the silver filling, even though years later, I now have the means to get it replaced. You can't tell unless you look very closely. Besides, it's a personal reminder of all my hard work.

The sacrifices extended beyond physical things too. Bootstrapping meant there was no money to hire a team, so we were entirely reliant on our own labor to keep the bakery doors open. At this point in our lives, Charles and I still had plenty of friends getting married. As gut-wrenching as it was to miss these precious milestones, sometimes we just couldn't physically remove ourselves from the daily operations of the store to attend. One wedding in Kentucky in which I was a bridesmaid meant I attended solo while Charles held down the fort. When our niece was born in Oklahoma City, we gazed at pictures of her for a year until we could finally hold her in person. Most people understood, but not everyone will understand the sacrifices you must make when you're building something, and that's okay.

The wait for that first location was excruciating, especially because it felt like one false start after another. There were some scary moments when I wondered if we were going to have to fold early. But we finally landed our location, and once we opened, we lucked out by being profitable very quickly. Part of the reason we were able to net in the black so soon is that we were running a lean and mean machine, and by that, I mean completely understaffed and overwhelmed with our immediate positive reception. Because of our rather unexpected initial success, Sprinkles was able to start paying back on our investment within the first year. But that didn't mean we were replenishing our bank account or buying that much-needed new car. Any profit that didn't go back into repaying ourselves went right back into the business. We had a ravenous business on our hands, and it needed to be fed. Money for equipment, more ingredients, more employees, an offsite office, a fancy website, fresh photography, graphic design, permitting and construction on new stores—the financial requirements for rapid growth were endless.

HOW DO YOU CHOOSE A FINANCIAL FUNDING RECIPE?

Being undercapitalized is the #1 reason companies don't make it. There are so many unforeseen challenges and delays when starting a business. Having enough money to get you through those bumps will mean the difference between giving up on your dream halfway through and being able to ride out the choppiness to smoother sailing. Fortunately, these days there are plenty of options for funding your dream company.

THE BIG FIVE

1. Bootstrapping
2. Friends, Family, and Fundraising

3. Incubators and Accelerators
4. Angel Investors
5. Venture Capital

BOOTSTRAPPING

Bootstrapping, or self-funding, means having enough money in your savings to get your company to a point where it's cash flowing and fueling its own growth. Entrepreneurs are optimists by nature, but when it comes to money, it's time to get very real. If you intend to bootstrap, you need to make sure you have enough money to see your vision through to the point where you become profitable. Cash flow is wonderful, but it's only part of the picture. There might be money flowing in, but if there's even more flowing out, then you don't have a self-sustaining business. Take the time to model out what you think you need to get your business launched and cash flow positive—and be conservative. It's like they say about construction (and take it from me, after close to twenty remodels): Everything takes twice as long and costs twice as much as you think it will. The same will be true for launching your business. And when considering the money you need to build your business, don't forget the money you need to live (even though it might be on freeze-dried ramen noodles). You could even consider taking on another job or side hustle or waiting to leave your full-time gig to keep money coming in during this time.

The benefits of bootstrapping are plentiful. You retain all ownership of your company, putting you in a position to receive all the proceeds from an exit event, such as a sale of your company. You maintain full control over your company's direction, being free to make autonomous decisions without outside or board counsel. Not to mention, you avoid spending the time, energy, and resources—pitch meetings, due diligence, regular investor updates—that is required when raising money! Not having to jump through those hoops affords you the ability to stay focused on operating your company and circumvent the dreaded situation of too many cooks in the kitchen.

The obvious downside of bootstrapping is that all the risk in this new venture is yours. While the glory is all yours for the taking, so are the failures. Bootstrapping is the stuff legends are made of; Apple (among so many great businesses) was founded in a garage. You must be scrappy and financially rigorous, which are celebrated skills for any founder.

FRIENDS, FAMILY, AND FUNDRAISING

If you can personally fund your company to a point where you're profitable, fantastic! But what if you don't have the money to even get your business off the ground? Bank loans—with the exception of SBA loans, which are bank loans guaranteed by the US Small Business Administration that require an unlimited personal guarantee—are generally out of the question for a risky new start-up, so now what? Well, that's what friends are for, right? Over one-third of start-up founders have raised money from friends and family. In fact, start-ups receive more than $60 billion per year from these investors. That's more than angel investors and venture capitalists combined. When you're raising money at the pre-seed or idea stage, what you're really selling is *you*—your vision, your experience, and most important, your grit and hustle. So, who better to do that than the people who know you best and believe in you? A loan from a friend or family member is a great way to get money at a low interest rate without having to give up any equity in your company. Alternatively, you could do a friends-and-family offering—via a SAFE or convertible note—to kick-start your venture. Both a SAFE (simple agreement for future equity) and a convertible note (debt that converts into equity at a future priced round) have become increasingly popular vehicles for funding an early-stage company. They save on legal fees by keeping terms relatively standard and by delaying valuation until a future financing round.

Typically, a friends-and-family round is composed of people who know and believe in you but who are not necessarily sophisticated investors. Make sure they are aware of the risks involved in investing and be sure to work with a lawyer for any agreement you make. It doesn't matter how close and casual your relationship is, your contracts should be formal and buttoned up. The goal is that—win or lose—you will still be able to enjoy Thanksgiving dinner with your family for years to come!

If your personal network of friends and family isn't fertile ground for reaping capital, don't despair. There could still be opportunity right in your proverbial backyard. Your customers have already proven with their pocketbooks that they like what you're selling, making them natural potential partners in your business. Tapping into this potential investor network is as simple as sending an email to your customer list letting them know you are raising money and offering them the opportunity to participate in the round at a minimum dollar amount. Converting your customers into equity owners provides precious capital and creates even greater brand affinity. As they now share in the upside of your business success, your customers will become an army of passionate evangelists.

Crowdfunding platforms are another great way to accumulate the capital you need with a larger number of small investments. Equity crowdfunding platforms, such as Republic, exist to democratize investment in private companies. This means that everyday investors (those without accreditation or a high net worth) can buy shares in your business with as little as $100. Other crowdfunding platforms like Kickstarter, Indiegogo, and IFundWomen offer access to cash without giving up equity but instead by providing a reward or perk. These platforms can also be a way for fans to purchase a product while still being developed in a presale.

Bobbie, a European-style baby formula company founded by two mothers, Laura Modi and Sarah Hardy, turned to crowdfunding in 2021 to allow their customers to invest in their rapidly growing company. In less than three hours, their campaign—dubbed The MotherLode—raised $245,000 and was ultimately oversubscribed. Having already raised $15 million in venture capital, the cash Bobbie raised via crowdfunding clearly wasn't the primary goal. Instead, both founders felt compelled to offer Bobbie customers a chance to share in the success of their business and to support a generation of women and mothers to become investors.

"Mothers are our reason for being, so mothers should be part of investing in our journey. We want The MotherLode to start a movement of a new kind of relationship between brands and their consumers, democratizing investing, and allowing mothers to invest in brands they believe in and use," says Laura Modi. Bobbie is part of a growing trend by start-ups to use crowdfunding, not just as a way to back their idea but as a creative way to democratize investments by allowing brand supporters to become real investors.

INCUBATORS AND ACCELERATORS

If you have a great idea or a nascent business that could use a boost, you might benefit from the assistance that an incubator or accelerator can provide. Incubators nurture a company from its earliest idea stage by offering education, mentorship, and access to valuable networks. Or, for companies that are further along, accelerator programs offer valuable training and networking intended to quickly expedite growth, as well as some financing in exchange for a small amount of equity. Though technically incubators and accelerators are focused on different stages of a company's life, these terms tend to be used interchangeably.

Y Combinator, founded by entrepreneur and venture capitalist Paul Graham, was the first accelerator program and remains one of the most prestigious, boasting Airbnb, Stripe, DoorDash, Coinbase, Instacart, and Dropbox, among others, as graduates of its program. Top accelerator programs, such as Y Combinator, are highly selective and involve an application process and interview to be considered. If accepted, you join a group or cohort of other start-up founders for a period to learn everything you need to accelerate the growth of your company. Most accelerator programs culminate in a demo day where founders pitch to a group of investors to secure an equity investment.

While many incubators and accelerators focus on technology companies, there are programs that offer support across many industries, including consumer packaged goods (CPG) and food and beverage.

Sephora, Target, and Whole Foods are all examples of retail companies offering this type of accelerator program. Greek yogurt maker Chobani offers an incubator residency for "innovative early-stage food and beverage startups," which Denise Woodard of Partake Foods attended. The program offers mentorship, access to Chobani's network of founders and retailers, and an *equity-free* grant to help companies scale and grow. Sashee Chandran, the founder of Tea Drops, bagless, organic, pressed tea "drops," credits the AccelFoods (now AF Ventures) food accelerator program with providing her with an important network of support early in her journey. AccelFoods took a small investment in Tea Drops at the time and then later in 2018 led a $1.9 million seed round. Tea Drops has seen massive growth since that time, manufacturing 7 million units in 2020 and securing an additional $5 million in financing (Series A) in 2021.

ANGEL INVESTORS

So you've tapped everyone you know, but your company is not the right fit for a venture capital firm. Now what? At this point you can consider raising money from angel investors. An angel investor is an accredited, or high-net-worth, investor who invests in start-ups at the earliest ("pre-seed" or "seed") stage. Unlike venture capital firms, angels invest their own money. Not that they aren't hoping for big returns just like VCs, but they have more freedom to write a check for something they might be especially passionate about since they aren't answering to other investors. Angel investors' checks can range anywhere from $25,000 to $1 million. These amounts can be significantly smaller when made by a large group of angel investors into a Special Purpose Vehicle (SPV), a financial instrument used to syndicate a large number of checks into one investment in the company.

The best way to find angel investors is through your own network. The investment community, like many, is relationship-based. Especially at this early stage in your company's life, when investors are betting solely on you as a founder, a "warm intro" will go a long way. Is your existing network limiting? I know founders who have gone "dialing for dollars" on LinkedIn. They looked up leaders in their industry and DMed them about their company and the opportunity to invest. However you approach it, just know that you will need to put on your sales hat. Raising money takes time and hustle!

HOT TIP

When seeking money from professional investors, such as angels and VCs, you will need to create a pitch deck to use as a marketing tool. A pitch deck is a brief PowerPoint-style presentation that gives an overview of your business and the investment opportunity. It covers many of the elements that we've discussed so far: the market size and opportunity, your product, founding team, revenue model, competitive landscape, financial projections, amount of money you are looking to raise, and how you will use those proceeds.

Sarah Kunst, founder of Cleo Capital, an early-stage fund, recommends using Guy Kawasaki's ten-page pitch deck as a model and gives my favorite advice on the topic: "Here's the thing about decks: Don't be ugly. Don't be ugly. Don't be ugly. The good news is it is free and easy to make a non-ugly deck. It is not 1999. You do not have to use clip art. You can go to Canva."

Know how much you want to raise, what you will use the money for, and how far it will take you. You also want to pinpoint an investor who will be the lead investor for your deal. This person is the anchor for your financing, negotiating, and setting the investment terms for all the other investors who join the round. They will take the largest piece of the investment offering, and their profile should be one that ideally gives other people confidence in the deal. Angels who have invested in companies with successful exits (one where they made a return, preferably a multiple, on their investment) begin to develop a reputation and carry a halo effect with them when they invest, causing other investors to want to jump into the deal too.

When considering which investors to approach, look for those whose investing thesis matches up with your business. Angels often have an area of interest that guides their investing. Some may also be led by a larger social mission, such as investing in underrepresented founders or environmentally responsible start-ups. Ideally you can find angel investors within your professional network, but there are also online platforms, like AngelList, that connect start-ups with angel investors. Ultimately, you are looking for more than just money; you want investors who believe in you, are aligned with your mission, and can offer help where you need it. Angel investors have typically had success in the business and entrepreneurial world and can provide valuable guidance, connections, and counsel.

VENTURE CAPITAL

If you decide to consider the venture capital firm route, it's helpful to understand how VCs work. Venture capital firms raise a fund with money from other investors (LPs, or limited partners) to make equity investments in high-growth companies, with the goal of making significant returns for those investors. So, you should consider venture capital only if your goal is to create a high-growth company—think compounding, not linear growth—that you intend to sell or take public in the future. VCs are not buy-and-hold investors. They lock in returns only when one of their portfolio companies has a liquidity event, such as an acquisition or IPO, and they generally have a seven- to ten-year timeline for that liquidity, which means they are also expecting speed. In fact, velocity is critical.

If venture capital sounds like the right fit for you, keep in mind that each VC firm, like most angel investors, has an investing thesis or mandate. Think of it as a lane that they choose to invest in; for some it may be a certain industry, and for others it might be broader reaching, like companies tackling the future of work. They also have criteria that guide their investing, such as investing at a specific phase of development and with a certain minimum investment or "check" size. As an early start-up, this will knock out most options initially because you will be too small for the checks that many of these VCs write, although there is a growing trend toward VCs investing earlier, "micro-VCs." Also, as part of an investment in a company, a VC will also establish a board to help guide the direction of the company, typically insisting on at least one board seat, which gives them oversight and some level of control.

Because of that, it's important to look for the right founder-investor fit. Remember my takeaways from cofounding Sprinkles with my husband? Many of the same lessons apply to the founder-investor relationship: It is a long-term commitment that should be based on trust and communication, and they will see you at your best and your worst. So, do your homework by asking tough questions, checking references, and making sure they can bring extensive knowledge and a deep network within your space.

A LESSON IN VC FUNDING

When Gregg Renfrew watched the documentary *An Inconvenient Truth*, back in 2006, she had no idea it would lead her to create a first-of-its-kind beauty brand. The film impacted her so much that she started making sweeping changes to her lifestyle to rid her home of harmful ingredients and products; from switching out household cleaning supplies to swapping plastic for glass, Gregg was on a roll. But one area that was hard to make significant changes to was her beauty regimen. Skin care and cosmetic products from the mass market to luxury brands were filled with chemicals of concern, but those branded as "eco-friendly" didn't perform as well as conventional products.

Late in 2010 and early 2011, Gregg recognized an opportunity in the market for a better, cleaner, and more thoughtful personal care and cosmetics line. She knew nothing about the beauty industry but felt compelled to act. So she partnered with two angel investors, partners in an entertainment law firm, and started to raise capital.

Now, this wasn't her first rodeo. Gregg had previously cofounded The Wedding List, an online bridal registry, which Martha Stewart acquired in 2001. Back when Gregg was building The Wedding List, she had a hard time raising capital because the male VCs she was pitching didn't take the billion-dollar-a-year wedding industry seriously. When it came to her new venture, Beautycounter, she was intent on building on her successes and learning from her mistakes. She pitched mostly to female VCs who understood the importance of her work and could amplify the brand but not micromanage the process.

When pitching herself and her new clean beauty brand, Gregg felt different in the room than she had with The Wedding List. Whereas she used to think of being a woman as a liability when raising money, she now felt empowered by it.

When it came to pitching investors, Gregg realized that she was interviewing them as much as they were evaluating her and her product. She mentally put herself in a powerful position by remembering that there is far more capital out there than good teams and ideas. "Cash is cash," says Gregg. "What can they do for you beyond writing a check? Investors need to bring more to the table than just cash. It's the partnership you form that's truly important. Will they back you up when things get tough?"

This time around, Gregg wasn't interested in getting her big idea off the ground with big VC money (though that would come later); she was focused on first finding honest, ethical angel investors who could amplify her efforts. She didn't want a group of people to act as a bank; she needed strong people in areas where she was weak and who had networks that could be accretive to her efforts.

"People get really caught up on valuation," asserts Gregg. "But you don't want to give away more of your company than you have to. Entrepreneurs fall in love with the headline of the valuation, and the higher the valuation, the more you must deliver at the end of the day. Investors will be expecting three to five times the return on their investment."

Her advice? Don't take the first money that comes your way or get glamoured by dollar signs. You want a realistic deal for you both to deliver on, and that won't handcuff you to a team that won't support or grow your company. Remember, there are a million investors out there but only a handful that are right for you. Don't settle for extra zeros when you could have excess long-term growth and, ultimately, more freedom.

GREGG RENFREW'S ADVICE TO FEMALE FOUNDERS READY TO PITCH THEIR IDEA

1. You got this! Dig deep and know you have the confidence to do this.
2. Use being a woman as an asset, not a liability. You're emotionally intelligent, so read the room.
3. Don't think about what you think you should wear to impress anyone. Wear the thing you feel good in, even if it's jeans. If you prefer, wear your hair up so you aren't tempted to play with it. Your physical comfort will translate to confidence.
4. Don't be apologetic—go on offense!
5. Remember, you know so much more about *your* business than anyone else, and typically, men aren't the consumers. It's widely studied that women have the purchasing power in the skin care and cosmetics industry; this means you will play multiple roles as the consumer and business leader, which you should leverage.

FOOD FOR THOUGHT

Unfortunately, all the dreaming and planning in the world won't get your business very far without capital. Luckily, there are plenty of options for funding a new idea. As you decide which path is right for your product, consider these questions.

How much capital will you need to launch your product?

Even if you have the liquid capital to bootstrap your business, do you have the resolve to take on all the risk yourself?

Do you have existing connections to angel investors or venture capital firms, or will you need to seek them out? If so, how will you do so?

Part Four

PROTECT IT!

Be Prepared to Lead, Defend, and Plan for the Future

About a year into our first store opening, there was still outrageous demand for our product. Even though we saw success on the shelves and in the books, it was hard to see it in our exhausted faces. I was still living most of my life sweating in the kitchen, hair tucked under an old baseball cap, as I frosted thousands of cupcakes a day. Aside from being physically demanding, the early days were an emotional roller coaster. Record days of sales would sometimes mysteriously be followed by much slower sales, feeding into my paranoia that our success was an anomaly, and it would all soon be over.

I specifically remember one day in October, waiting for the typical hordes of people to show up, and it ended up being one of the slowest days on record. I started to panic. *Has everyone decided they're over us? Are we just a flash in the pan?* I naively soon realized that it was Yom Kippur, one of the holiest days of the year for Jewish people that involves a twenty-four-hour fast. We quickly learned to track and record the ebbs and flows in our business so we weren't caught by surprise with thousands of excess cupcakes or, conversely, left with nothing to sell by midday. I don't know what it is about the end of daylight savings, but customers go into hiding for about a week! Valentine's Day is nuts . . . Halloween not so much. Gradually things started leveling out, but that feeling of paranoia, that fear that competition was nipping at our heels, that customers were fickle, that we needed to innovate and stay relevant and defend our business—*that* feeling never goes away. Maybe it was irrational, or maybe it's true that "only the paranoid survive," but it's what drives any business leader to do everything within their power to *protect* their business.

What is a leader? What does one do all day? Whether it's while holding the title of president, CEO, or even still founder, it's a lofty, aspirational role that, beyond being a public figurehead, can often feel like an enigma. The truth is, it's a lot more work and responsibility than signing checks, showing up to board meetings, and smiling at events.

A leader oversees a company's overall growth plan, strategy, and vision. They are ultimately responsible for growing and protecting the business. On any given day, a leader must innovate, protect against competition, defend against distracting new projects to remain laser-focused on goals, and secure the right financial partners and opportunities. The success or failure of the company rests on them. And, until there's a real leadership team in place for delegation, everything falls on their shoulders. They're on the hook when the website goes down or the head baker calls in sick.

I remember one crazy Valentine's Day, when customers were wrapped around the block. To meet the more-than-ten-times-normal demand that day, we were making batter at an off-site commercial kitchen and delivering it throughout the day in refrigerated vans. Well, Charles was. I was still inside the kitchen frosting as fast as I could. He had rented the van for the day and in a harried moment, accidentally locked the keys inside. With hordes of hungry customers waiting to pick up their Valentine cupcakes—there was, in fact, a black market wherein customers who didn't want to wait hours in line were offering customers leaving the store with their cupcakes a hefty markup—and all our product locked away in our rental van, Charles put on his do-whatever-it-takes hat, pulled a golf club out of his car, and smashed the windows. A true leadership move. Soon enough, that batter was being delivered to the back of our bakery to be baked into pretty cupcakes. And we lost the security deposit on that van.

Although a leader is the captain of the ship, they are beholden to a lot of people—from employees to investors—and, if you choose to assemble one, a board of directors. A captain charts the course but, unless they can effectively communicate their vision to employees and guide them to reach these goals, the ship isn't leaving the dock. The same goes for securing the right financial partners, ensuring there's runway and liquidity to get to the intended destination.

When it comes to leading a business, sometimes the titles of founder and CEO or president go together, but not always. As the founder you will have to decide where you fit into leadership depending on your strengths, as your business grows. And, though the title of CEO might seem like the highest point in the organization, it's not always the smartest decision to hire yourself for the job, just to remain at the very top. In the case of Sprinkles, Charles and I were cofounders, but he assumed the official title of CEO because he is an incredible manager and leader. Though we had both been tasked with CEO responsibilities throughout our time building the business, our growth eventually pushed us to crystallize roles. I could have tried to give myself the title because it sounded great, but I knew it was not what I wanted or what would be in the best interest of the company.

If you are a cofounder, you will need to make that same decision. If you don't think you're the person for the job, and want to stay firmly in the founder role, you can elect to bring in a CEO—if you don't happen to have a business partner who is a natural fit, as I did. This can happen right off the bat or at a later stage in the company's life to help lead the next phase of growth. Sometimes at a critical inflection point in growth, investors will encourage or force a founder to leave the CEO post behind. This doesn't always go according to plan. The most famous of these cases is, of course, when Steve Jobs was fired from Apple in the 1980s and then came back to build Apple into one of the world's most legendary companies.

Though, let's be honest, most founders are not Steve Jobs.

In this next, and final, section of the book, I'll walk you through many of the events, responsibilities, and considerations that will occur on your company's growth journey that force you, as a founder, to grow into your role as a business leader, whether that ever translates into an official title.

Step Eighteen

TURN UP THE HEAT
ON THE COMPETITION

*Trademark your brand, consider your
company type, and defend your IP.*

came up with the idea for the name *Sprinkles* coming back from a visit
to Charles's family in Oklahoma. We were connecting through the
Dallas/Fort Worth airport and, I know it sounds strange, but I had a
semi-vision of my cupcake shop named "Sprinkles" in the food court.
Not that my initial concept had anything to do with fast food, but my
premonition hinted of a business so widespread that you would see it in
airports across America. The name emblazoned across that little storefront felt aspirational—sprinkles literally sit on top of the icing of the
cake, and it was just fun to say. How could I go wrong?! Turns out, when

it comes to protecting your business, a lot can go wrong. And I didn't learn how much until we were already full steam ahead.

But before I learned a few hard lessons, one thing I did know was my first step—make sure the name wasn't already trademarked by another bakery. Amazingly, it wasn't. It was only registered for children's clothes and a couple of other things, but unbelievably not for a bakery. What were the chances?!

Of course, as I mentioned before, I could have easily named my business Candace's Cupcakes. The alliteration alone was tempting enough, and I already had an established customer base who picked up their orders from my West Hollywood apartment. But I wanted my business brand to be bigger than my own personal brand. And, at that point, I wasn't even thinking about a personal brand. (Was it even a thing in the early aughts?) I just wanted to create something that didn't exist before. Plus, even from the get-go, I was thinking long-term. What would Candace's Cupcakes mean someday if I were to sell the business and no longer be associated? Sprinkles it was!

ALL ABOUT THE *K*

Many years after launching Sprinkles, I learned about the prominence of the letter *K* in top company names. Some researchers believe that, historically, the best brand names have at most two syllables and at least one "exotic" letter, like an *X* or a *K*. Believe it or not, this is how Nike got its name. And Sara Blakely deliberately incorporated the *K* sound into the name of her company Spanx. In *Bloomberg Businessweek*'s "Top 100 Global Brands Scoreboard," half of the top twelve have the *K* sound. Consider Coca-Cola, Microsoft, General Electric, Nokia, McDonald's, and Hewlett-Packard.

REGISTERING YOUR BUSINESS NAME AND BEYOND

There is magic in the right name, but finding the perfect name for your business doesn't stop at landing on one you like. It requires a thorough search to ensure your name is free to use. Yup, business names aren't all free for the taking.

First, you'll need to check at the state level. Performing a business entity search through the database on your secretary of state's website is quick. Next, you'll need to ensure there won't be any trademark disputes at the federal level, by searching the US Patent and Trademark Office (USPTO) online database for trademarked business names that are like yours. The key here is that no one is using your name in the industries in which you choose to operate. For example, Sprinkles was in use for children's clothes, but not for bakeries. However, it's a good idea to think about what businesses your company might branch into in the future. For example, when Sprinkles moved into making and selling ice cream, we ran into an issue in one state where there was an existing frozen yogurt business named Sprinkles. Even something as simple as ice cream can be complicated and need legal intervention.

And, to confuse things further, just because there's not a trademark for a certain name doesn't necessarily mean you're in the clear. Much like a long-term partnership could be eligible for the same rights as a married couple, common law dictates that a business can claim a trademark solely from operating in a geographic region for a certain period—whether officially trademarked or not. To help prevent that situation, a preliminary Google search will always be a solid temperature check. Depending on what comes up in your search, you will have an immediate sense of whether there is an existing business active in your field with the same name.

Of course, securing a business name is just the beginning. These days, starting a business is also about finding one that allows for a decent URL and social media account handles. As entrepreneurship grows, industries get more crowded and competitive, which means you might have to get creative. It's almost impossible to find a single word in the English language with an available .com domain name. In response, new businesses have embraced silly, nonsensical names. Consider Mmhmm, a digital camera application used to create virtual rooms, backdrops, and presentations during video conferencing calls. If you are effective at worming your way into your customers' lives, however, your zany name will be endowed with its own meaning. Just think how surprisingly normal it sounds these days when you tell someone you're going to "Venmo" them or hop on a "Zoom."

DRESS TO PROTECT

Not long after Sprinkles opened in 2005, word of our little cupcake bakery and the lines it inspired had spread far and wide. Soon, the attention became hard to ignore—literally, it was in our faces. People began visiting our shop with professional long-lensed DSLR cameras, with the intention of documenting our product, our presentation, and as much of the process as possible, in hopes of replicating our business idea. We started fielding crazy phone calls from aspiring entrepreneurs threatening us to let them franchise or else they were going to challenge us with massive competition. In fact, at one point, while leaving work at the end of the day our baker was approached for the red velvet recipe in exchange for $100 cash as though it were a back-alley drug deal! All this to say that if you create something valuable, get ready, because competition and sometimes blatant thievery are sure to follow.

There's not a lot you can do to prevent this. Of course, we guarded our recipes carefully and we did implement a rule that there was no photography allowed in the store. (Can you imagine a business doing that in today's Instagram-hungry world?) But beyond that, once you've secured the name and begun building a brand identity, it's critical to register your name, your logo, and any other distinctive trade dress components. Trade dress refers to how you "dress" your product, which can include everything from the shape to the packaging of the product or even the display. Trade dress goes beyond the mark of the logo, indicating the unique visual way a product attracts customers and differentiates itself against competition. For an element of trade dress to be eligible, it must be nonfunctional and inherently distinctive. For Sprinkles, that was our modern dot decoration that sat on top of every cupcake. Very quickly it became innately associated with Sprinkles Cupcakes and distinguished our brand from all the rest. So we applied for and were granted trade dress protection. No one else selling cupcakes could legally use our modern dot decoration.

Because Charles and I had experience working with technology companies who rely heavily on intellectual property rights to protect their innovations, we approached our business through that lens, but many people don't. True, it may all seem costly both in time and money up front, but it's part of the foundation you are laying to set your business up for future success. And it pales in comparison to launching a business that you then must rebrand down the line. Now *that* can get expensive. Don't worry; you aren't expected to know any of this. A good trademark attorney can help guide you through this entire process.

But why go through all this trouble? If you don't register your brands, logos, and names as trademarks, you may not have the right to use them. What's worse, you may not find out until you have been operating for a while and sunk tons of money into marketing materials and advertising for your business. Also, if you are looking for funding in the future, having the proper trademarks—and patents—is an important piece that investors will look for.

You want a trademark to protect your brand and to be able to bring legal recourse if another business infringes on your trademark. Venture capitalists often talk about a "moat" for your business. In other words, what is going to protect your business from invaders—that is, competitors? With a bakery, unlike a technology company with proprietary intellectual property (IP), there really aren't any barriers to entry. So how could we protect all the work we had put into our venture? We worked with what we had. Our modern dot decoration was distinctive and was intricately associated with our brand. It was one of the few design elements that distinguished our cupcakes from the rest. Sometime later we realized we should try to also trademark the cupcake display we invented with our architect. The sliding trays with cupcake-sized die-cut holes, which sat at the exact right angle for optimal viewing, were completely unique to our stores. However, when we tried to trademark the design, we were told that it was already the ubiquitous standard for the industry. Other bakeries had copied it so quickly and mercilessly that we were too late to protect it!

I'll be honest, trademark protection is the not-so-fun-and-glamorous part of protecting your business. But your brand has value only if you protect it. Very soon after opening we started to see cupcake bakeries with stores that looked exactly like ours, cupcake bakeries that used the word *Sprinkle* in the name, as well as those who used our modern dots. We were determined to prevent massive confusion in the marketplace. So we relied on cease-and-desist letters to let people know when they were infringing on our trademarks. We didn't want to do this; every letter cost us time, money, and stress. But we had created something valuable and felt strongly that we needed to protect it.

I want to highlight that this tactic wasn't anticompetitive in nature. We knew there would be competition, and we were right. Cupcake shops were popping up everywhere. Frankly, though annoying, it really was a sign of success. But we couldn't allow businesses to piggyback on the goodwill we had created through our name and decorations and then potentially damage it. Most bakeries didn't have the same standards of quality and presentation. If someone walked into a bakery covered with dots, and thought they were in a Sprinkles, their bad cupcake or customer service experience could be confused with ours and ultimately hurt our brand.

Not only was working offensively expensive, but it also forced us to face trial in the court of public opinion. And, not in a favorable way.

Here is a *sprinkling* of headlines that ran in the *Los Angeles Times* business section over the years:

- "A Point of Cupcake Contention," August 21, 2008
- "Sprinkles Set Off a Tempest in a Tin Pan," September 4, 2008
- "Cupcake Kerfuffle: Sprinkles Settles Trademark Infringement Case" February 8, 2012

Even though we were a mom-and-pop business, we were definitely painted as the big bad guy. When the first article was written, we only had two bakeries!

This type of trademark protection works both ways. For example, when we opened Sprinkles at Disney World in 2016, we realized that three modern dots could easily and cleverly mimic the silhouette of Mickey Mouse. We thought it was a genius cobranding move, a way to celebrate the storied character and act as an ode to our new landlord. We even went so far as to paint the design on our store wall. Unfortunately, Disney's lawyers did not think it was quite as cute as we did and made us repaint the wall. This was a good reminder for us that not every intellectual property infringement is malicious; we earnestly thought we were promoting the great Disney brand, but even with the best intentions, we were unintentionally trespassing on Disney's IP.

Though it wasn't applicable to Sprinkles, no conversation around intellectual property would be complete without touching on patents. A patent grants an inventor exclusive right to their invention, protecting it from being used by others for a certain period. Entrepreneur Pree Walia filed and secured eight patents in the process of building the Nailbot and launching her business Preemadonna, which powers creative expression through interactive smart hardware. Preemadonna's flagship product is Nailbot, a beauty device for Gen Z makers and artists. It's a connected, at-home manicure device that instantly prints on nails any photo, emoji, image, or self-created design in five seconds. Preemadonna has eight granted utility patents and many more that are pending. One of the most exciting and daunting moments for an entrepreneur can be filing your first patent. Here are some things Pree wishes she knew when she first started her patent process for Nailbot:

1. **Make sure you file a provisional patent.** You can file this yourself. It can give you a placeholder of close to a year to file a full utility patent. You can file additional provisionals as well that have new material not covered in the first provisional.

2. **Find an attorney that understands your product and the bigger vision of your venture or company.** Bigger firms may give you a deferment on payment, but smaller boutique firms or solo practitioners often give you more personalized and adequate support. Don't forget to factor in the costs of office actions, filing fees, maintenance fees, and so on when

making your decision. Ask your counsel about the overall cost—not just the filing and initial preparation costs.

3. **It may take a while.** Patent protection helps you if you play a long game to bring your product or service to market. It often takes many years to get through the examination. If you are in a rush, try filing a Track One for prioritized examination with the USPTO for your utility application. It limits the number of claims you can submit, but you'll get a faster response.

4. **Figure out which markets you want coverage in.** If your strategy is just the United States, you will save a ton of legal expenses. If you want coverage in other markets, make sure your counsel keeps you in the loop on all the charges, translation fees, maintenance fees, office actions, and so on. Sometimes it may not be worth it to pursue an international approach, and the same counsel that was a fit for the United States is not the right fit for international markets.

5. **Focus on building your company and launching your invention!**

You may think patents are only for tech companies, but that is just not true. Designer John O'Donnell, of the West Coast surf-prep brand Johnnie-O, patented his hidden shirt button design called the Tweener Button. Frustrated by the fact that sometimes having two buttons open at the top of a men's shirt is too laid back, but one often feels too buttoned-up, John started incorporating the Tweener, a hidden button and placket in between the second and third buttons. It gives you the comfort to unbutton the second button. Menswear crisis averted and protected.

MAKE SURE THE BUSINESS IS OPERATING ABOVE BOARD

Beyond protecting your intellectual property through trademarks and patents, you'll need to consider the business holistically. If you're starting any small business, you need to decide on how to structure and register it as an entity, legally speaking. This will all depend on your personal circumstance, and the goals you have for your small business. Factors to consider are tax and liability implications, as well as the amount of paperwork required. I highly recommend looking into each option thoroughly and seeking out guidance from other business owners, your accountant, and legal counsel. Here are the most common types of business structure, from a high-level perspective:

Sole Ownership

If you are going into business for yourself as the only owner, there are two options:

- **Sole Proprietorship:** This is the easiest way to incorporate from a tax perspective—the business and individual are treated as one, so you do not file separately. The downside is that you can be held personally liable for any of your business's liabilities. If your industry is at low risk for any liabilities, this might be the fastest, cheapest, and easiest route to take.
- **LLC (Limited Liability Company):** An LLC will protect your personal assets from claims against the business, including lawsuits. Most small businesses operate as an LLC. Profits and losses "pass through" the business to the LLC owners, and it is not taxed separately like a corporation.

Partnership

Partnerships are the simplest structure for two or more people to own a business together. There are two types:

- **General Partnership:** In a general partnership, profits and losses get passed through to the partners, who also assume liability for the business's debts or obligations.
- **Limited Partnership:** A limited partnership is the right path when there is a mix of general partners and limited partners who are investors only and have no control or liability. This type of partnership requires a lot more filing and paperwork but will depend on stakeholders.

Corporation

A corporation is an entity that is entirely separate from its owners. It offers liability protection, business continuity, and easier access to capital by allowing for a sale of stock. However, with a corporation, you must have a board of directors.

- **C-Corp:** With a general corporation, one downside is that it gets taxed separately from the shareholders, which means it gets taxed at the corporate level, and then again at the shareholder level. However, this is the preferred choice for investors and if you plan to go public one day.
- **S-Corp (Subchapter Corporation)**: An S-corp allows income or losses to be passed through on individual tax returns, like a partnership. This is best for a smaller corporation, with one owner and less than one hundred shareholders.

FOOD FOR THOUGHT

As you dive further into your planning, it's critical to make sure your business is buttoned up from a legal perspective. Whether you're on the precipice of launch or you've been scaling up and are ready to make things official, consider these questions:

Have you made sure that your desired business name is available to use?

Do you have a trusted legal partner or attorney to guide you?

What are the necessary trade dress elements that you need to secure?

What structure makes the most sense for your business entity?

Step Nineteen

NEVER STOP EXPERIMENTING
IN THE KITCHEN

Increase your edge with innovation.

Five years into our Sprinkles journey, I became pregnant with our second son. Late one evening—well into that pregnancy—Charles and I returned home from a party and all I wanted was a cupcake. Not just any cupcake—one of *my* cupcakes. I was customer zero, after all. Despite having almost constant access for years, I still devoured them with gusto. It was a common occurrence for me to be spotted grabbing dark chocolate Sprinkles Cupcakes at parties. Friends would laugh at the irony that I was surrounded by my own baked creations all day long at the store and still couldn't help myself after hours. But that's what happens when you create a product you love. People were amazed that I wasn't sick of them. And no time was that truer than during both of my pregnancies. On this evening, I was well into my third trimester and the craving was intense and only a Sprinkles dark chocolate cupcake would do. Easy enough, right? Well, not exactly. I had already eaten all the cupcakes at the house (yes, I kept a stash at home), and it was well past Sprinkles' closing time.

So, I flopped my very large self on the bed to pout, turning on the latest *Breaking Bad* episode from my DVR. But, instead of paying attention to whatever illegal business Walt and Jesse were getting themselves into, I started to vent. Out loud. To my husband. You could blame it on pregnancy hormones, but in retrospect, I'd like to think it was pure genius expelling itself. Now, it probably came off a bit more like dramatic whining about the irony that, despite owning a cupcake shop, I couldn't get my hands on a cupcake whenever I wanted. It may not have been my finest moment, but the accidental brainstorm surely paid dividends. Literally!

Instead of simply dismissing the idea as impossible, my husband and I started playing with ideas and what ifs. What if you could get a cupcake at any time of night? If you did, then you could monetize twenty-four hours a day. We were already paying rent twenty-four hours a day for a storefront but only open for a portion of that. This went on and on . . . until we landed on it. Yes, it was late at night in the middle of a pregnancy-driven chocolate cupcake craving that the idea for a cupcake vending machine was born. The lesson? Always be open to the "crazy" ideas, because that's what the most innovative ideas look like at first glance.

At this stage, Sprinkles was expanding rapidly and continuing to be blessed with incredible buzz and demand, but our high profile and success meant we also had competition nipping at our heels. We knew we needed to keep delivering on our original mission to meet our customers' expectations, while at the same time putting forward new ideas to delight them in unexpected ways. No one wants to be a one-hit wonder, especially in a city like Los Angeles.

So, we forged ahead with our idea. It took a couple of years to go from late-night brainstorming to a working model, but in the meantime, we got down to business with the important stuff, like an original jingle. Yes! We were very serious about the sound that would emanate from the machine, so we hired a composer to create the music that plays anytime you buy a cupcake from our machine. It's sweet and pop-y with a rapid-fire rap of all our flavors and, like any good jingle, it's a total earworm—once you hear it, you can't get it out of your head.

Shockingly, when we were finally ready to bring our newfangled device to the world, several local media outlets shot down our pitches to cover the launch. No one was interested. Charles and I had wholeheartedly embraced this nutty idea of a twenty-four-hour cupcake machine, but no one else seemed to see the genius in it. And so, one spring day in 2012, we simply took down the construction barricade hoping someone would care.

Soon enough, pedestrians happened upon it, a few posted videos on social media, and just like that, the match was lit. Within hours, we'd received dozens of calls from media outlets around the world, and news film crews were fighting each other for space on the sidewalk to be the first to officially break the story of this sweet innovation. Media hadn't liked our pitch, but now that it was a legitimate news story, they all came flocking.

Where was I when all this was going down? Sitting at the judges' table on the set of my Food Network show, *Cupcake Wars*. I desperately wanted to be a live witness to all the mayhem developing in front of Sprinkles but had to settle for watching my phone in between takes. And I watched in awe as the Cupcake ATM inspired one news hit after another. Within hours, someone's video demonstrating the Cupcake ATM had received hundreds of thousands of views (Yes, I was kicking myself that it wasn't a video Sprinkles had filmed), and the tweets just kept on coming.

Our weird little invention wasn't just the internet conversation du jour, it also became the ultimate punchline for some very famous late-night comedians like Jay Leno and Craig Ferguson and inspired a "Top 10" list by Dave Letterman. The Sprinkles Cupcake ATM even had its fifteen minutes of fame on hard news—Wolf Blitzer of CNN reported on it in his nightly show! And it made it into the plotlines of TV shows such as *2 Broke Girls* and *Bunheads*. That "crazy idea" became a media sensation, tourist attraction, significant revenue driver, and incredibly prescient form of contactless delivery. Today there are twenty-six Cupcake ATMs around the country, with many more to come.

KEEP IMPROVING ON THE RECIPE

So how do you become a master of innovation without devoting massive amounts of time and resources you don't have? Although innovation can seem like a heady concept, it simply means that you are improving on what exists. Innovation doesn't have to come from a dedicated product development team with a big budget. In fact, the best innovations have historically come from scrappy start-ups who "move fast and break things," to quote the Facebook slogan. Your lack of structure is, in fact, your superpower. It keeps you agile, and the fact that your back is up against a wall daily means you are already a champ at solving problems creatively.

Don't be intimidated or discouraged by the idea of incorporating innovation into your business. It could stem from a brainstorming session with your coworkers, a suggestion from a customer, or even an idea you borrow from another industry (the way I staffed my bakers throughout the day to manage inventory and keep our cupcakes extra fresh was borrowed from the just-in-time production technique the Japanese pioneered in the seventies for making cars!). It can also come simply from personal frustration, like my late-night prenatal cupcake rant. The key is to stay open and curious to new ideas and possibilities, as well as cultivate a corporate culture where ideas are appreciated and open exchange is welcomed by both employees and customers alike. Innovation is, after all, a mindset.

The Cupcake ATM was born of just this sort of creative thinking, which I then utilized to identify additional ways to push the boundaries of Sprinkles' offering. Still, years after the *Oprah Winfrey Show* debut, there existed a pent-up, unfulfilled demand for our cupcakes on a national level. Our brick-and-mortar expansion was innately slow, and shipping flew in the face of my promise of a freshly baked cupcake—to be enjoyed on the day it was baked. So, to capitalize on all this excessive hunger for our product, I developed a line of cupcake mixes to bring the freshly baked

Sprinkles experience into home kitchens across America. As I've mentioned before, we partnered with Williams Sonoma to bring Sprinkles to the masses. I did this by translating the top Sprinkles flavors into a dry mix using the same ingredients we used at our bakeries, such as Nielsen-Massey vanilla—but in powder form—and Callebaut cocoa, to which the home baker would then add the perishable ingredients to create a dozen Sprinkles Cupcakes. The sleek canister even included twelve of our signature modern dots so the resulting batch would be unmistakably branded. This new product was sold at our bakeries, as well as hundreds of Williams Sonoma stores across the country, increasing our reach exponentially. Not only did it offer a solution for the thousands of customers who wanted to try Sprinkles and couldn't get to one of our stores, but securing shelf space at a beloved national retailer was also a natural way to introduce the brand to those who hadn't yet heard of us.

We also took Sprinkles on the road—literally—in the form of a Sprinklesmobile. Concurrent with the rise of Twitter, there was a new type of food truck on the scene. An update on the old-school food trucks created to feed construction workers on the job, this modern-day food truck was a foodie experience—one worth the pilgrimage. The Sprinklesmobile was part of this pioneering wave, and in typical Sprinkles style, it was also a design experience. We transformed a Mercedes Sprinter van into a Sprinkles store on wheels, designed by our award-winning architect and realized by the same car customization experts that were the subject of MTV's *Pimp My Ride*. The shiny chocolate-brown van sported modern dot wheels, and the side of the van opened to reveal our signature die-cut trays holding rows and rows of freshly baked cupcakes. The Sprinklesmobile started rolling out to film sets, movie premieres, birthday parties, and various street corners around town. We kept Angelenos abreast of its location via tweets throughout the day, and workers stuck in offices across Los Angeles finally had a way to conveniently fight that late-afternoon sugar slump. The Sprinklesmobile also road-tripped across the country to support new store openings and as the subject of one of our employee Maureen Bharoocha's short Sprinkles films.

There was a line out the door at our bakeries. Sprinkles was highly profitable and showed no signs of slowing down. We could have rested on our laurels, baking cupcakes and serving customers all day long from our stores alone. We didn't have excess time or workforce to devote to non-mission-critical initiatives. But innovation is indeed critical for staying ahead of the competition. The adage "Innovate or die" speaks to the defensive significance of innovation in a highly competitive market. Sprinkles had been a trailblazer as the first-ever cupcake bakery, but with the proliferation of cupcake bakeries, the landscape had drastically changed, and we were now one in a crowded pack. We felt compelled to raise the bar again, to maintain our position as an industry pioneer and to keep competitors at bay.

Innovation can be applied to marketing techniques as well. We harnessed the explosion of social media in the form of Twitter and Facebook to market the brand in new and playful ways. We developed a "whisper word" tactic that we were able to leverage in several different ways. The way it worked was if you whispered the word you had seen on Twitter or Facebook at the cash register, you would get a free cupcake. These customers felt part of a special insiders' club sharing a secret with the cashier. Plus, people would show up and oftentimes buy more. As a result, the campaign helped increase loyalty and sales among an already devoted customer base. Additionally, it boosted our online following and drove customers into the stores during slower times of day. We also used Twitter and Facebook (during the now outdated chronological algorithm) to announce the fleeting appearance of flash flavors.

Even better, it was a great way to make use of excess cake batter and frosting. While we started creating off-the-menu flavors, we quickly had fun experimenting, giving stores a list of approved combinations, while also taking suggestions from store employees for new combinations we hadn't tried yet. With cake, frosting, filling, ganache, coconut, and sprinkles, the combinations were endless, which offered a secondary benefit of being able to test out new flavors. We offered the experimental cupcakes for free to people via social media by inviting them to be exclusive "taste testers." When they showed up, they got the cupcake along with a form to fill out on the spot with their thoughts about the cupcake. Free focus group testing, while surprising and delighting customers!

We were also able to take advantage of trending online or local top-ics, like sporting events, to make our whisper words resonate even fur-ther. For example, if the Dodgers won that evening's game, customers could jump on a BOGO (buy one get one). And, in all these ways, social media became this amazing lever we could pull whenever business de-manded it.

It may be hard to believe now, but Facebook back in the day was truly a social platform, in the traditional sense of the word *social*. People used it mostly to keep up with friends and family. We were one of the first brands to realize its powerful potential for engagement and sales on- and offline. Sheryl Sandberg, COO of Facebook, used Sprinkles as a great early example of a business using Facebook in innovative ways. Imagine, one of the most powerful and innovative companies the world has seen citing our little cupcake bakery as innovative. *That* is the power of thinking outside the box.

INNOVATE FOR A HUNGRY MARKET

A little over ten years ago, Lauren Gropper was working as an environ-mental designer focusing on sustainable building design. Transitioning from city centers to Hollywood set designs, she couldn't help but notice something on her craft service lunch breaks—plastic. From foam takeout boxes to plastic bottles and utensils, Lauren started to consider how much ephemeral waste was created on set every day. "Why are we us-ing expensive and toxic materials like fossil fuels to create products we only use for five minutes?" she wondered.

Having studied sustainable design, she instantly recognized this as a design problem. Single-use products had a definite place in our modern world, but they needed better, more sustainable, and less toxic design. This is when she launched her company, Repurpose.

Innovation could have become her middle name as she made the leap into creating a first-of-its-kind product: compostable single-use pa-per and plastic tableware. It seems like a no-brainer now, but when Lau-ren first began exploring and testing new materials, this concept was completely novel in the marketplace. Now, a decade later, the consumer world has caught on to the devastating effects of single-use plastics on our planet and bodies and is hungry for better alternatives. This rise in education has been great for elevating the Repurpose brand and its products but has given way to new competitors in a space where Repurpose formerly occupied all the territory.

Aside from catering to the general consumer market, Repurpose sells to wholesale customers like Whole Foods and Target, who are always looking for the next cool product to house on their shelves. "It's a delicate balance of piquing retailers' interest with new innovations, while also pushing the core products you know will drive growth," Lauren explains. "Even if you've been a trusted supplier for years, you're constantly competing with new emerging brands and products edging into your shelf space."

Sometimes that results in an innovation created purely on the defense to protect your business and secure the brand in the hearts and minds of consumers. For example, Lauren made the decision to create a paper straw, not because it was particularly innovative or what felt exciting, but because there was a competitor moving into their existing product's space.

At the same time, it's important to keep innovating to push the brand's vision forward. "For us, it was disrupting a product people used every day—trash bags," says Lauren. As a result, the product development team tinkered with materials, what they looked like, and how they worked. Today they are the market leader in eco-friendly, compostable trash bags.

"We looked at what was in the market, identified what we could do better, and used our brand equity to bring it to life," remarks Lauren. Repurpose's innovation strategy always comes from a place of materials and function. They don't try to disrupt how people use products, but rather how they're made by improving upon an already ubiquitous item. "I admire the changemakers who are disrupting whole systems, but we've been successful with the lens of improving on what is already there," says Lauren.

For Repurpose, innovation has become a more formal process because it's centered around materials and technology. It's one thing to innovate for innovation's sake in order to maintain consumer interest and generate buzz, but for Repurpose, it's more intentional and takes a serious investment in time, planning, research, and testing. "We focus on materials and how they are disposed of. We are constantly exploring new materials and debating the risk of taking a chance on new technology, versus creating it ourselves," Lauren explains.

"I'm a big proponent of not letting perfection become the enemy of good, but that's almost impossible in our industry. We don't have the luxury of putting a product into the market, getting feedback, and then iterating from there. If we put a failed product into the market, consumers will associate this poor design with our brand and never try us again. It's difficult when you only get one shot," Lauren says.

Much of this is unique to the sustainability space, where products often undergo rigorous scrutiny and a certification process. So, Lauren has a few tips for those of you looking to innovate sustainably:

LAUREN'S TIPS FOR ENTREPRENEURS INNOVATING WITH SUSTAINABILITY IN MIND

Timing Is Everything

You want to be ahead of the curve to carve out your share of the market before it gets too saturated, but being too early has its disadvantages too. If you're a pioneer, there's a lot of unforeseen time, energy, and budget that goes into educating your customers. When you set out to disrupt a market, or bring innovation to a category, do your market research to determine if the mass market is ready or soon could be ready for your product. Oftentimes the consumer doesn't even realize that the product or service could exist, so education and awareness will be critical to success, and both require a significant investment.

Consider Entire Systems or Single Tools

Hitting the right timing in disrupting a market is critical, but understanding how is just as important. Consider if your consumer would be ready to adopt a new form of behavior at this moment. Are they ready to shift an entire behavior pattern, or would you find more success by focusing on improving upon the tools within the system? As consumers become more educated and interested in overhauling established lifestyle systems, this type of model will surely be the next wave of sustainable business, which involves thinking through a bigger picture that connects to innovation of materials, usage, and disposal toward a truly circular economic model.

Perfection Is the Enemy of Sustainability

When innovating for sustainability, you must let go of the idea that you can be perfect. It's impossible to launch with perfection when the gold standard is a moving target. From manufacturing and impact to marketing and packaging, this is a world where you can never do enough. Technology and legislation are rapidly changing, and you don't want to be stuck with technology that can be easily replaced or restricted in five years.

Sustainability is a long, imperfect game where you'll get further by listening, learning, and educating, rather than lecturing and making inflated claims. You can't be perfect, so don't claim to be, or you'll open yourself up for some rather uninvited hole poking. In sustainability, you're trying to take a 100 percent stance, and it's mathematically impossible to do so on every front.

The Big Takeaway

Ultimately, the biggest takeaway is that you can't think of your product or brand as the solution. Green design and technology are a massive, complex industry, and climate change is a monumental issue. You will find the most success when you can adopt the mentality and messaging points that you are not the solution but rather one small, very essential part of it.

FOOD FOR THOUGHT

Though the day-to-day grind of entrepreneurship can often become all-consuming, as a founder, it's important to continue to create and innovate to delight your customers and keep the competition at bay. Ask yourself these questions:

Are you staying open and curious to new possibilities to cultivate an innovative mindset?

Do you have a culture of innovation among your team, or should you formalize the process of brainstorming and innovation at your business?

Are there technologies or materials that are being introduced that could inspire a new innovation for your business?

Is the timing right for a given innovation? In other words, will your current audience be receptive to this idea immediately, or will they require education?

Step Twenty

KEEP YOUR COUNTER SPOTLESS

Stay focused on your goals.

I t's very easy to fall in love with—and even become addicted to—the creative invention stage of entrepreneurship. As founders, we are so adept at spotting opportunities that we see them literally everywhere. Having a brain that's always noodling on the next thing is an advantage when you are thinking about innovation, but it can lead to disastrous distractions when working toward a long-term goal.

Building a company isn't like TikTok, with a euphoric hit every twenty seconds. Building something takes time and, even in small entrepreneurial companies, always takes longer than anticipated. Investors look at the horizon of a start-up investment as typically seven to ten years before expecting to see any sort of liquidity event. So, patience, focus, and commitment are qualities that will be critical for running that marathon, even though you're itching to sprint. As tempting as it may feel, you have to deny the creative impulse to jump into something new to keep executing against your established goals.

I SCREAM. YOU SCREAM . . . MAYBE WE SHOULDN'T HAVE SCREAMED FOR ICE CREAM.

A few years into Sprinkles, the retail space next to us in Beverly Hills—formerly a popular burrito spot—came up for lease. We were bursting at the seams, particularly in the kitchen, where our employees were frosting elbow to elbow. Luckily, we all really liked each other, but something had to give! We knew we needed the space in the back to expand the kitchen. We could easily blow out the wall and stretch our legs (and arms) a bit.

But what about the street retail? What could we do with the front? A new project! A blank canvas! My mouth was salivating for the opportunity to create from scratch again, and equally excited about the prospect of developing something delicious and nostalgic—right in the Sprinkles brand sweet spot. My palate and childhood memories led me to ice cream. My high school days had been marked by high-quality American ice cream. From Ben & Jerry's to Steve's Ice Cream, where they smashed treats into decadent ice cream against a marble slab (yes, a Cold Stone Creamery predecessor), it was the heyday of American-style ice cream. Unlike much of the ice cream made today—which starts with a mix typically absent of eggs because that adds an element of difficulty and expense—this was high fat and made with eggs, which gave it heft, chew, and very little air (or *overrun*, as they say in the biz).

But that was years ago, and since my own coming of age, the market had turned its back on ice cream in favor of frozen yogurt (or fro-yo, if you're a true aughts diehard). Okay, there was some minor excitement around gelato, but nothing could compete with Tasti D-Lite, Pinkberry, and those local neighborhood self-serve spots that seemed to pop up everywhere. It was in the middle of this low-cal dairy craze that I somehow became obsessed with the idea of bringing back rich, fatty, American-style ice cream in all its glory.

Typical.

We decided a sweet little scoop shop next door would be the perfect companion to cupcakes. We would make our own old-fashioned ice cream, which would organically become an extension of our cupcake brand, with the ability to marry the two products. Think blending butter-cream cupcakes right into the ice cream, sandwiches with dark choco-late cupcake tops, and sundaes padded with red velvet. What started as a whim suddenly landed us in the ice cream business, building an en-tirely new product, complete with a new educational curve working in dairy to go with it. Unless you've worked in the ice cream business, you probably wouldn't realize that making and selling ice cream requires totally different health codes, permitting, and display than any other food service.

We opened to mobs and lines of Sprinkles and ice cream fanatics. The product was phenomenal, and we expanded the concept into sev-eral different markets. Our instinct had been spot-on; it was time for American ice cream to make a comeback. Yet, being on the cusp of a new trend meant we were quickly met with competition that took the assignment and ran with it. Our product was new, but also buried within our existing brand, which made it impossible to catch the wave of buzz these other breakout names were riding. We were also met with the challenge of the popularity of inventive, unconventional flavors. Staying true to the Americana spirit, we remained traditional in our flavors, rely-ing on the cupcakes to add an unexpected twist. However, the media thrives on something new and unique that shocks or surprises, and while we developed our own cult following, the ice cream never found a large fanatical audience. All the ice cream stores have since closed.

Although developing Sprinkles ice cream was creatively rewarding, and I'm incredibly proud of the product we made—to this day, I still re-ceive DMs from hopeful Sprinkles ice cream fans asking me when the stores will reopen—I know we took our eye off the prize. We had an in-credible thing going with our cupcakes.

There was insatiable demand around the country for Sprinkles. Our stores were packed, and the business model was an efficient machine. People would come into the store and leave with two or three dozen in five minutes. Compared to an ice cream model where people would come in, try samples, and twenty minutes later leave with a scoop, it was hard to compete against ourselves.

Ultimately, even though the product wasn't necessarily a failure, our commitment to the original brand mission was, for a period, all in the name of love—of creating. We were enamored with our new project because we were missing the novelty. It was a fun, creative distraction versus delivering on the original mission to build out Sprinkles Cupcakes, which was a more plodding, operational challenge. With the time we spent on ice cream, we could have opened more cupcake stores and sent lots more dough to the bottom line. The lesson is that as fun and tempting as it is to head off in a new direction, stay the course.

THE POWER OF "NO"

Patrick Herning is the founder of not one, but *two* rapidly growing start-ups. He founded his size-inclusive luxury brand, 11 Honoré, in 2016, and then in 2020 he cofounded the beauty-inclusive platform Thirteen Lune with cofounder Nyakio Grieco (see step 9). At the helm of two mission-driven, venture-funded companies, there is no one who needs to remain more on task.

Patrick says, "Disciplined focus is key to navigating the early stages of a start-up. For as much as testing at a high volume is critical, what is equally—if not more—important is having the focus to say *NO*."

He's learned that saying no is one of the best things a founder can do. "You identify your key pillars that drive the business and commit to only activating around initiatives that move those pillars forward," Patrick explains. "It becomes your personal guardrails to stay on track. Now, I am the king of NO, and it has never served me better!"

STAY FOCUSED ON THE RECIPE

That lesson extends to everything that comes your way. One minute everyone is ignoring you, and the next everyone wants to talk to you. You'll naturally want to say yes to everything when the smartest thing to do would be to say no to almost all of it. The opportunities become greater, but the focus needs to get smaller. Saying yes to something means saying no to something else.

What does it mean to stay focused? It means truly understanding where you stand and where you are going. It can be easy to get pulled in many directions in the thick of it, but you need to periodically step back and zoom out.

Luckily, we had seasoned mentorship within our own Sprinkles family. Charles's father, Chuck, had a background in strategic business planning, having been trained at IBM Corporation and then CEO of three different corporations, where he was tasked with developing a strategic direction and plan for growth. In watching us struggle to find our next move, he realized that this discipline could not only be appropriate for large corporations but also—perhaps even more so—for start-up companies finding their way without much of a long-term plan. This belief proved true as he started his own consulting company and developed business plans for an array of industries from sugar refining to banking to automobile dealerships.

Chuck loves this quote by Peter Drucker: "Efficiency is doing things right. Effectiveness is doing the right things." He had the sense that—while successful—Charles and I were running around aimlessly. As he learned early, the question is not if you are working hard, but what are you getting done. He saw us managing the daily crises from moment to moment—which wasn't going to set us up for long-term success.

Chuck could see this, even when we were too in the weeds to realize it, and offered to fly out to LA to conduct a planning session. We had no idea how we would find the time to escape the store for a *whole day,* but we staffed as best we could and kept our phones close by. Chuck set up two large flip chart easels in our living room and we settled in for a long day. He was able to take us out of the mire and up into the sky by plainly laying out—on those big pieces of flip chart paper—where we were, where we were headed, and what obstacles were preventing us from getting there.

Chuck's planning strategy was to list and prioritize every significant hurdle we were facing and then try to identify the underlying cause. For example, the biggest challenge we were facing during that first session was in sufficient output. We just couldn't make enough cupcakes to meet demand. But this was merely a *symptom* of other problems, such as a need for bigger mixers, more production space, and better inventory management. Chuck challenged us to assign a number to each component of the issue: If we needed to make x number of cupcakes, what size mixer should we buy, should ingredients be delivered, and what size kitchen could accommodate this new volume. Putting numbers on goals as much as possible takes the emotion out of things and allows those goals to be measurable. Quantifying our goals helped remove the emotion from decision making and allowed those goals to become measurable. Together, we determined an action plan that held us accountable in terms of who had ownership and in what timeframe. Our first planning session was so clarifying that we made a point of doing one every year. These sessions were invaluable.

CHUCK'S COURSE-OF-ACTION CHEAT SHEET

A plan is a course of action that does the following:

- Defines goals
- Sets objectives
- Identifies obstacles
- Quantifies tasks
- Obtains commitment
- Assigns responsibility
- Maintains agreement
- Schedules activities
- Measures progress
- Documents results

He credits the incredible training he received at IBM for the way he approaches strategic planning with companies. As an IBM salesperson, he needed visibility into his clients' business goals and objectives to market the right computer systems, so he encouraged them to develop a documented plan for their future. If he couldn't do his job without clarity, how could they? Having a business plan, once you're well established, is the most efficient way to get to your goals.

FIVE WAYS TO STAY FOCUSED

Prioritize Your Time

There are myriad time-saving methodologies. Try a few out and see what is most effective for you. Here are a handful to consider:

- *Eat That Frog* maintains that tackling your most important task first each morning helps you move the needle right away, which sets your whole day up for success.
- David Allen's *Getting Things Done (GTD)* system starts with writing everything down to clear your mind and dividing your to-dos into more manageable action items.
- The Ivy Lee method involves creating a to-do list the night before with only six items, which you attack in terms of priority, moving on to the next one only when you've fully completed the first.
- Time chunking is the practice of breaking your day into chunks of time without interruption to be more effective and ultimately more productive.

Delegate Tasks

The ability to effectively delegate is one of the most important skills a great leader can possess. It can be hard to let go—trust me, I've been there. But if I hadn't hired and taught a team to replace what I was doing at Sprinkles, I could never have grown my company beyond its original location. Delegating may seem like more work at first (because it is), but it will pay dividends when you are freed to focus your energy on the most strategic initiatives.

Delegate effectively by matching tasks with the right skill sets and communicating your expectations clearly. Your team will benefit from the trust you have placed in them, and the energy you give to their development will keep them engaged.

Practice Saying No

New York Times bestselling author James Clear maintains that the ultimate productivity hack is saying no. Consider the economic principle of opportunity cost I wrote about in step 6. When you say yes, by default it means you are saying no to something else. Remembering this will help you weigh what is truly important to you and spend your time accordingly. Saying no can be very hard for people.

If this is you, find a way to say it in a tone that feels comfortable. You can even come up with a stock email with prewritten language, so you don't have to sweat over saying no each time. Maybe something to the tune of "I would want to give this request my full attention, but my schedule doesn't allow for it right now."

Also, keep in mind that a *no* doesn't have to mean never. It can be *not yet.*

Take Time-Outs

Easier said than done, but time away and time for play is invaluable to the busy entrepreneur. If you think that's frivolous, you need to change your mindset or face the consequences down the road. There's an epidemic of burnout in entrepreneur culture, and it stems from the always-on, always-plugged-in, always-working nature of work today. True, some of this is par for the course when you're starting a business. But whatever time you can pull away to let your mind rest and play will pay back in both productivity and creativity. Don't believe me? Even Albert Einstein espoused the benefits of play. When he was stuck on a certain problem, instead of powering through, he would take time away to play his violin. He attributed some of his biggest breakthroughs to this practice.

Track and Measure

As biohackers like to say, you can't hack it if you don't track it. They're referring to wearables such as Oura Rings and blood sugar monitors to measure the health effect of your choices to optimize them, but the same holds true for your business. Every company should be tracking key performance indicators (KPIs) on a regular basis. A key performance indicator is a metric you measure regularly, as in weekly, to help narrow your focus and stay on top of your most important business goals.

KPIs will vary depending on the business. For Sprinkles, we cared most about the number of cupcakes sold, number of customers, average customer spend, and sales per square foot. But the KPIs for an app would be the number of downloads, amount of time spent on the app, or engagement. Once you determine your KPIs, you will want to set up a KPI dashboard, which is a reporting tool that brings all these metrics together in one place for easy tracking.

FOOD FOR THOUGHT

Innovation can propel your business forward, but it can just as easily become a roadblock. As you grow your business, be mindful of where your focus lies. If you find yourself off the path, ask yourself these questions to get back on track:

Is your current focus aligned with the original business goals?

Have you established your company's KPIs? Do you need to revisit or revise them?

Do you have any person or entity that can hold you accountable? If not, is that something you can implement to keep you focused?

Step Twenty-One
SAVE ROOM FOR THE NEXT COURSE

Prepare for your next stage of growth.

t was a surreal moment. Seven years after opening the doors to Sprinkles, I found myself on the other side of the table from a group of private equity investors discussing a significant investment in my business. Not so long before, I had been in *their* seats, among the bankers advising founders on their upcoming liquidity event. My dream for Sprinkles was for it to become a great American bakery brand, and that dream had not wavered. What had changed was my belief that Charles and I should be the ones to shepherd it all the way there.

Sprinkles had become largely an operational challenge and we were increasingly aware of the skill set required to run a company at this scale—now an internationally recognized brand with a national footprint.

To take our company to the next significant stage would take seasoned operational expertise, as well as an infusion of capital. I knew what we had to do, ready or not. I owed it to my cupcakes.

A significant investment, acquisition, or successful exit is the dream of many founders. If you've taken on angel or VC money, it is also an expectation. A liquidity event gives early investors the return they seek on the money they have invested in you. To be fair, when I opened Sprinkles, I had no idea I was about to embark on the trajectory of a high-growth start-up, so I had no reason to think my cupcake business would ever see a liquidity event. This is to say that any small business that's successful can become a desirable investment or acquisition target. So, what are the most likely future exits or outcomes for your company?

HOW TO GET YOUR
BUSINESS OUT OF THE OVEN SAFELY

Strategic investment

An infusion of capital, by venture capital or private equity, can propel growth, as well as the opportunity to take some money off the table. Beyond capital, private equity firms can help with strategic guidance, governance, and a vast network of relationships.

Acquisition

An acquisition can take the form of a financial (private equity) or strategic (another company) buyer for either equity or cash. A strategic buyer will often pay more for your company because of the synergies they realize by acquiring your business. If they are interested in expanding into a certain product, market, or category, and you help them do that by saving them time and money from developing in-house, it holds additional value for them. The acquisition can made using cash, equity, or a mix of both. Taking equity means you're betting on the prospects of the parent company. A financial buyer is buying to realize a return on their investment later so they might not pay as much, but with their network of connections and industry expertise, they could add a lot of value. Also, you don't have to sell 100 percent of your business. It's possible to retain partial ownership.

Merger

Merging with another similar-sized or similarly valued company because it's accretive and helps both companies be more competitive is an option. If the company is publicly traded, you immediately have liquidity. Merging with another private company might not technically count as an exit but could give you scale and get you there eventually.

IPO

Taking your company public means selling shares on the public market to raise funds and supply liquidity to early investors. This means your company has reached a certain scale and predictability in revenues. While it is a very prestigious milestone to reach, it does come with heightened visibility and a lot of additional accounting and reporting requirements, as stipulated by the Securities and Exchange Commission (SEC).

Bring on a CEO

Another direction you can go is to bring on a seasoned CEO to take the reins, relieving you of much of the day-to-day leadership and oversight. This doesn't mean you won't be involved, but it does afford you the opportunity to step into another, perhaps more advisory role or focus on an area of the business that suits your strengths or interests. In some cases, this may happen as part of another exit event, such as an IPO. Founder/CEOs can also be voted out by their board or investors if they lose voting control of their company.

WATCH OUT!

A void finding yourself suffering from "founder syndrome," where founders refuse to give up control, even though their company has outgrown their leadership. This dangerous territory will ultimately start to limit the growth of the entity.

ESOP (Employee Stock Ownership Plan)
With an ESOP, the retiring owners will sell the company to their employees. You can also do a buyout, which will pay out over five years with a certain amount of earnings.

Stay the Course
You can also make the decision to stay at the helm, continuing to make your company profitable, to reinvest the profits back into your business to grow. At a certain point, you can take those profits and divide them among your investors in the form of a dividend.

● ● ● ● ●

If you could never imagine being separated from your beloved company, that's totally normal. Nothing says you must make an exit, and you can certainly keep executing without giving a thought to leaving. But it is important to consider how much of your personal net worth is tied up in your business. As any financial advisor will tell you, diversifying your portfolio is the key to being able to sleep soundly at night. Charles and I had given everything we had to our business—most of our adult working lives, as well as all of our finances. We didn't own a house or anything with substantial value beyond Sprinkles, and if something went awry all our net worth could have disappeared. Although our business was going gangbusters, we felt it was a prudent move to consider selling a stake in Sprinkles to take some money off the table.

We hired an investment bank specializing in mergers and acquisitions in the consumer space to help us look for a strategic or financial investment or acquisition. We spent six weeks preparing a book with all the details of the business, financial, marketing, and projections, to present to all interested parties. After soliciting potential interest, which entailed sending books out to those who signed NDAs, we set up meetings with all interested parties. Then, offers were submitted. We considered several offers, chose the terms and financial partner we liked best, and began negotiations. It took five months from the final LOI (letter of intent) to get the documents signed, conduct due diligence, and prepare the legal documents to complete the deal.

Entering an investment deal is just like any relationship—it's all about finding the right match. We ultimately landed with a private equity firm who understood and appreciated our brand, and who possessed a depth of expertise in the restaurant and retail sectors. They've since grown Sprinkles from eleven to forty locations by expanding with more Cupcake ATMs and stores with smaller footprints. They've been able to bring in experienced leadership and make changes like moving the headquarters to Texas, expanding the product mix with chocolates and cakes, and offering nationwide shipping. They have also begun to franchise to seasoned operators, with the goal of expanding the footprint not just nationally, but internationally.

HOW WILL YOU KNOW WHEN IT'S FULLY BAKED?

Remember, the role of a parent is to raise little birdies to fly away. It may be melancholy, but, ultimately, it's a sign of a job well done. If you decide that is the path you want to take with your business, you might be wondering when the right time is to do that. Simply put, it's when your business is going well. Ever heard the phrase "Leave on a high note"? It's true! The best time to shop for a suitor is when you're on a great growth trajectory, the market is healthy, and industry trends are in your favor. You may think that the financial markets are logical, rooted in numbers, but they can be subject to trends too. Certain industries and types of companies go in and out of favor. Although it can be hard to step away when things are going well, it will be the best time. If you have products or projects in the pipeline you believe will add significant value to the company, you might want to hold off to make sure you are getting paid for the full value of what you have created before leaving. Of course, if someone will pay you now for what you're going to do in the future, then the time might still be right.

How do you know what you're worth? Determining the value of a publicly traded company is relatively straightforward—it's what the public markets dictate. From day to day, it can be easily calculated by multiplying the stock price by the number of shares outstanding. Quantifying the value of a private company is inherently less simple but can be done in a variety of ways. The most common method, comparable company analysis, involves gathering data from a group of publicly traded industry peers to produce an average multiple that can then be applied to the financials of your company. This multiple can be of any number of metrics, including but not limited to sales, earnings, subscribers, or other relevant data points.

You should also be aware that there is a relationship to the growth rate of the company and industry, as it relates to the size of the multiple. Fast-growing companies and industries will be at the higher end of the valuation range than those that are growing more slowly. Technology companies, for example, are generally valued at higher multiples than brick-and-mortar retail businesses because of the velocity with which they can scale. It's helpful to be knowledgeable about the valuations and market activity within your industry, although private company valuation is something best left to the experts. Ultimately, however, your business is worth what someone will pay for it.

REESE WITHERSPOON: HOW TO MAKE A SALE WITHOUT CALLING IT A WRAP

Reese Witherspoon has more than earned her place as a major player in Hollywood. After all, she's been in the business for most of her life. A rising child actor, she became a household name after she brought the iconic Elle Woods to life in 2001's *Legally Blonde*. She went on to win an Oscar in 2006 for *Walk the Line*, but even still, she struggled to find satisfying roles in Hollywood. In 2011, Reese read one terrible script that left her fed up. How could such blatantly misogynist stories still be allowed to dominate the industry? She called her agent to vent and was shocked to be told that every actress in Hollywood had been dying for the part.

At some point, Hollywood had decided that women weren't the audience for films and stopped developing movies with women as the central characters. Reese knew this wasn't true, nor was it right. This is when she became determined, more than ever, to change the narrative for women. Reese's husband, and biggest champion, observed that she read more books than anyone he knew. Maybe she should start optioning books that showcased the type of storytelling she craved.

So Witherspoon self-funded her own production company called Pacific Standard and began devouring book galleys to find female-centered stories to bring to the screen. She produced *Gone Girl*, *Wild*, and the first season of *Big Little Lies*, all based on books she loved, but even after three consecutive hits, it was challenging to keep her company afloat. She asked, "How could I make this into a bigger, farther-reaching, scalable endeavor?"

With ambitions for a new type of media company Reese knew she would need outside investment, and ultimately found backing from Peter Chernin's Otter Media. In 2016 she relaunched her new company as Hello Sunshine. While her mission to tell female-led stories remained unchanged, the scope of her new company grew far more expansive. In addition to Reese's Book Club, Hello Sunshine creates content across multiple platforms, including scripted and unscripted television, feature films, animated series, podcasts, audio storytelling, and digital series.

For Reese, selling a portion of Hello Sunshine five years later wasn't intended to reduce her role in the business. It was a strategic move to help further the company's directive and spread the ethos to even more people, with her still at the helm. Hello Sunshine courted several offers. A majority stake was ultimately bought by a new media company backed by Blackstone Group and led by former Disney executives Kevin Mayer and Tom Staggs.

The valuation and sale of Hello Sunshine landed around an impressive $900 million for a production company with only four films and six television series under its belt. However, what Hello Sunshine lacked in volume, it more than made up for in the data. Every film and show they produced was proven to be a top driver of user engagement for subscribers who were new to the shows' respective streaming platforms. Engagement means more subscribers, which means more recurring revenue, which means streamers want more content produced by Hello Sunshine.

Selling Hello Sunshine didn't mean losing anything. Quite the opposite, in fact. The cash infusion was intended to help them grow exponentially. "We doubled down on our mission," Reese says. "This sale gave us the ability to tell more stories, to hire more female filmmakers, to promote and lift up even more authors."

Reese continues to oversee Hello Sunshine's day-to-day operations and participates on the board. And, of course, she's still actively engaged with her community on social media—especially Reese's Book Club.

FOOD FOR THOUGHT

Though making an exit is the last thing on your mind when you're launching your business, it's important to consider. If you happen to have a clear idea of where you want to end up, it can dictate so much about how you start. Take a moment to envision the future and ask yourself these questions:

What are your goals for your company? Will you eventually need outside funding or support to get you there?

Are you building a business with the intention of eventually selling?

How much of your net worth is tied up in your business? Is it time to devise a plan to diversify your finances?

Conclusion
SERVE IT!

had been fully immersed in my business night and day, for years. Every waking hour was spent marketing it, working *in* it, working *on* it, and fretting about it. Every non-waking hour was spent dreaming about it. It was my entire identity.

It was also the one topic everyone wanted to talk about with me—from my dentist to the Uber driver to *every* dinner companion I've ever sat next to. Not only that, but millions of people had also watched me for over one hundred episodes on the internationally syndicated *Cupcake Wars*. I was officially the "Queen of Cupcakes" who had founded the world's first cupcake bakery. By the end, it was hard to distinguish where Sprinkles started and I stopped. Until one day it wasn't. Weird.

My entire self was so intertwined with my business that when I was no longer operationally involved, I felt a bit unmoored. In fact, selling the majority of Sprinkles and walking away from the day-to-day was a difficult personal transition for me. Though it was disorienting, I knew it was still the right move. It was prudent to diversify my investments and I yearned to be more present for my family; and truthfully, Sprinkles needed someone else to take the reins to help it scale. Still, I was unprepared for how long it would take to untangle my own identity from my business. Overidentify much? Thank goodness I *hadn't* named it Candace's Cupcakes. I can only imagine how hard *that* would have been.

EMBRACING THE *AND*

I n A. A. Milne's fictional forest, Winnie the Pooh is only Winnie the Pooh. Tigger is just Tigger, and Eeyore remains Eeyore, day and night. They each have their "one" thing—honey, bouncing, moping. In our twenty-first-century reality, however, we can be, and have, more than one thing. One day we might feel as fired up as Tigger; another we might feel as despondent as Eeyore, and yet another we might just want to sit down with a honey jar (or a box of Sprinkles). And this is beautiful. We get to embrace the *and*s in our lives. For so many years, I was searching for my "one" thing at a time, from a career in banking (am I a finance person?) to a small Beverly Hills shop (am I a pastry chef? an entrepreneur?) into which I could pour all of my attention. But I've realized I can have my hands in multiple honey jars. We're multifaceted humans, and it's okay to embrace different qualities, engage in various interests, and share them all with the world. The answer to my searching is: Yes. I am a businessperson and a pastry chef and a founder and a writer and a mom and so much more. Sure, it's helpful for our brains to focus on one task at a time, but we live in an age where we can be anything and everything. So, fly your *and* flag high! And the next time you find yourself grousing, remember that the following day, you have the chance to Tigger yourself all over town.

So, what did I do next? I leaned into all the domestic pursuits and parenting extras I hadn't yet had a chance to fully enjoy. That meant helping more at my boys' school—with classroom parties and volunteering for school events. I was able to be there for every pickup and drop-off. Our family set down permanent roots—something I had sought my whole life—by buying a house and renovating it to create the perfect place to raise our boys, with room to play. I took a beat to give myself uninterrupted time with my family and to recalibrate. It was a special time, and I was incredibly privileged to have the freedom to do it. But, of course, it didn't last long.

After building my bakery into a national brand, the furthest thing from my mind was jumping right back into the food business. But sometimes life just happens to you no matter how much you try to keep it at bay. Cut to a warm evening in the backyard of my friends Chris and Caroline O'Donnell's home. Yes, Chris O'Donnell as in Robin from the Batman franchise and crime-fighting Special Agent G. Callen on *NCIS: Los Angeles*. Beyond his career on the big and small screens, Chris has a passion for wine and a deep appreciation for great food. Having recently installed a wood-burning oven in their backyard, he and his wife started hosting regular pizza nights for friends and family. These gatherings quickly gained a reputation for being the place to be on Sunday night. On one such evening, I bit into my first slice of pizza and paused, my head spinning in delight. Pizza had always held a special place in my list of food loves, and I had tasted my fair share from around the globe, but this was something special. I raced over to the oven to meet the creator of this magical pie.

When I met Daniele Uditi, a pizza chef who had emigrated from Naples, Italy, my love at first bite was reaffirmed. Daniele had grown up in a family of bread bakers and brought this sensibility to his pizzas. It was meant to be; we were united in our love for dough. What's more, Daniele had a huge sweet tooth and was an avid Sprinkles fan. I spent the rest of the party next to the oven chatting with Daniele, learning his story of coming to the United States with just $300, his grandmother's sixty-year-old dough starter, and some very big dreams. There was a time when he was so broke he had to sleep in his van at Venice Beach, but he remained determined to make it in America. I was so struck by his talent, passion, and drive that when he mentioned that he would like to open a pizza restaurant someday, I couldn't help but blurt out, "Let's do it!" The result is Pizzana, a neo-Neapolitan pizza restaurant that has garnered numerous awards, including the Michelin Bib Gourmand, with multiple locations in Southern California and now Texas and growing.

WHAT MIGHT BE NEXT FOR YOU . . .

Start Another Company

Itching to get back in the game . . . immediately? Of course you are! You were a born entrepreneur, and now you're a seasoned founder. You can take everything you've learned from your first business and do it better the next time.

Invest in Other Start-Ups

Being a founder is exciting . . . and downright difficult. Being an angel investor is a great way to keep some skin in the game, with less lifting. Plus, you get to invest in companies that speak to your passions, which can be so exciting and rewarding.

Become an Advisor

If you're not necessarily in a place where you want to build businesses with capital, there are other ways. Helping founders doesn't always mean investing your own money. You can commit your time in the form of mentoring or joining the board of a growing start-up.

Take a Nice Long Vacation

A friend, who successfully exited his vitamin company, was deluged with a multitude of new opportunities but decided to take time off from the working world. He understood that with his next opportunity, he would likely be devoting the next decade of his life, so he is being very choosy with his next move to enjoy time with his young daughter.

· · · · ·

Building on your experience in a single industry by capitalizing on expertise and existing relationships can be a very powerful way to leverage past success. But, as much as I adore the food world, I also relish expanding my knowledge base and diving deeper into new areas of interest. This is what happened with Play 2 Progress, an early childhood development platform Charles and I cofounded with Dr. Allie Ticktin, an occupational therapist with a specialty in sensory integration.

Allie had come into my life when my children were just babies and toddlers. She cared for our boys from time to time while getting her master's, and then doctorate at USC and I was able to witness her passion firsthand. Since completing her doctorate, Allie had developed a special sensory-based methodology for working with children through play to help them thrive emotionally, socially, and physically. As a mom of two, I understood how deeply parents want to do the right things in those critical first years to build the best foundation, but they don't always have the proper knowledge or tools. I felt compelled to help bring this special method to a broader stage so more parents could encourage their children's development in the right way. Charles and I partnered with Allie to create the Play 2 Progress brand and launch a developmental platform. Play 2 Progress now has two busy play centers in LA, a book, and digital courses with plans to leverage its proprietary methodology through licensing and franchising.

The most rewarding thing about building a company is that you're able to pass along all the valuable lessons you've learned to others. And, when you don't have to wear all the hats at once, you can choose which hat you most prefer to wear (and looks the best on you). I love donning my marketer hat with Pizzana and Play 2 Progress. And I especially love guiding these talented founders to "take off their aprons," step out from behind their businesses, and help make their personal stars shine. Some of my personal branding efforts have yielded some exciting things: I cocreated and executive produced a food competition show on Hulu, *Best in Dough*, where Daniele stars as a pizza judge. I helped shepherd Allie through the process of landing an agent and a book deal, as well as helping her secure local TV segments, podcasts, and collaborations to grow her profile as a thought leader in the early childhood space.

As much as I embrace the identity of entrepreneur, being one can be exhausting. Because I don't have endless energy to keep cofounding companies (even though I might want to) I have begun actively angel investing in female and underrepresented founders of early start-ups. I love it. Being an investor is like coaching and cheering from the sidelines instead of playing on the field. You're invested in the outcome, but it's not up to you to win or lose the game. I strive to be a value-add investor, contributing more than just capital, but also supporting and amplifying with my influence, connections, and advice. Most importantly, I'm continuing to stay curious and be open to opportunity, as well as surrounding myself with people who are actively doing and creating things to move our world forward.

But this is all food for thought for another day in your future. I've come a long way, and so will you. As you preheat your oven, gather your ingredients, and prepare your recipe, remember that the convection fans of reality may blow your passion sideways as it rises. But as long as you keep your trays spinning, your dreams will bake to perfection, and you will reach your very own sweet success.

ACKNOWLEDGMENTS

When I was in second grade I wrote a book titled *Reach for the Stars*. I bound it with a row of staples and illustrated it with stick figures stretching their skinny arms up to a starry sky. At just seven years old I was already steadfast in my belief that the world was full of possibility and that the only true path in life was to follow your dreams. This could only be possible because of the optimism and encouragement instilled in me by my parents. Mom and Dad, thank you for always telling me I was capable of anything I set my mind to and for impressing on me the values of integrity, intellectual curiosity, and hard work. And to my little sister Brooksley who has the biggest heart and is the most passionate cupcake person out there. I love you guys!

Charles, you leaned in on a crazy cupcake idea when you could have safely kept marching up the corporate ladder. Thank you for joining me on the adventure of a lifetime and for being my perfect partner in *all* things. Your wisdom, kindness, and humor have always had my heart and I'm so lucky to be on this journey with you. Thank you for believing in me so completely. I love you so much!

To my boys: Charlie, I was eight months pregnant with you during the Sprinkles Dallas opening, and Harry, you were flipping sugar-fueled somersaults in my belly on the set of *Cupcake Wars*. Both of you have had seats on this start-up train since your earliest beginnings and you both possess the out-of-the-box thinking (and sweet tooth) to show for it. I love it when you weigh in on business issues your dad and I grapple with at the dinner table and when you say you want to be entrepreneurs when you grow up. I can't wait to see what you create. I love you both more than you'll ever know!

To my in-laws: Chuck, thank you for supporting all our ventures over the years with your strategic vision and towering whiteboards, and for allowing me to share your genius process on these pages. Thank you to Lynda for always doing what needs to be done, including counting cash and folding boxes—you are a saint! Thank you both for befriending countless strangers and converting them into customers. You have always been our best public relations team and we love you!

Nothing at Sprinkles would have been possible without our employees. To Sprinkles' superlative team of managers, assistant managers, cupcake associates, bakers, frosters, drivers, and order line associates, your passion was the heartbeat of our company. I am profoundly grateful. A special shout-out to some of our early Sprinkles family: Mirian, Nicole, Vineet, Stephen, Jason, Alexa, Emily, Delmy, Sergio, Jerson, Dustin, Ellen, Jay, Leah, Maureen, and Celeste, just to name a few. Thank you for all the fun!

Thank you to our many Sprinkles customers for including us in your lives—from your most special celebrations to the everyday ones. It has been an honor to share those moments with you.

Thank you to the committed team that has continued to lead the Sprinkles vision since we took a step back several years ago: Allan and Chris at Karp Reilly, Dan Mesches, and Julie Masino. Your passion for the Sprinkles brand has exceeded all our expectations.

Thank you to our CN2 Ventures rockstars: Bobby, Nicole, Vineet, Andrea, Daniele, Troy, Dagny, Dustin, Allie, Oak, Kun Che, Regan, and our outstanding teams at Pizzana and Play 2 Progress. We couldn't do any of this without you.

Thank you to my writing partner Heather Sundell. What a blessing to work with you. You are a gifted creative *and* business mind, which makes you an actual unicorn. I am so grateful that the world (well, Darcy Cobb) brought us together. I love your prose and I trust your counsel. Beyond the pages of this book, you have encouraged me to embrace my diversity of interests, given me a deeper appreciation for the millennial perspective, and made me a more confident writer.

Thank you to my partners at Harper Collins Leadership. To my publisher, Sara Kendrick—I knew my book had found its home when I met you. Thank you for giving me this beautiful platform to share my story and for shepherding me through the process with patience and wisdom. To my editor, Linda Alila, thank you for your deft eye for detail—what a pleasure to work with you. Thank you to Sicily Axton and Briá Woods for your marketing expertise and to Jessica Smith for the inspired interior illustrations. Ron Huizinga, thank you for capturing the soul of my book with your cover. Thank you to the team at Neuwirth & Associates: Jeff Farr, Aubrey Khan, Beth Metrick, Mikayla Butchart, and Noah Perkins.

Thank you to the team at WME. Richard Weitz, you are a true friend and a wizard at what you do. Thank you for helping to guide my career through its various twists and for making sure I am always cared for at WME. I adore you for your gigantic heart and for always telling it like it is. Thank you to Julia Bodner, who is the best agent and human, period. Your energy supercharges me—I am so lucky to have you on my side. To my literary team at WME, I will sound like a much bigger fish than I am by naming you all but I'm so grateful to Sabrina Taitz, Margaret Riley King, and Haley Heidemann for seeing me through the bewildering process of writing, selling, and marketing a business book. I would not have made it to the finish line without your wisdom to lean on. Also, a big thank you to Andy McNicol, who got this project off the ground.

Thank you to the amazing entrepreneurs and experts who shared their experience and advice on these pages. I know how precious every hour is when you are running a company and I am so appreciative of the time you spent with me. Your stories and insights are an inspiration and I'm honored to share them in my book: Reese Witherspoon, Gregg Renfrew, Denise Woodard, Meredith Melling, Valerie Boster, Gail Becker, Nyakio Grieco, Patrick Herning, Lisa Odenweller, Jesse Draper, Annie Campbell, Alli Webb, Auzerais Bellamy, Shiza Shahid, Lauren Gropper, Pree Walia, Audrey Wu, and Sashee Chandran.

Thank you to my mentors in the venture and investing space—Sarah Kunst, Amy Griffin, Anna Doherty, Jesse Draper, Linnea Roberts, and Maxi Kozler. You live your values out loud. Thank you for showing up for women, including me. I have learned so much from you.

Thank you to the wonderful women of WieSuite. To Dee Poku, who sensed a need and quickly banded a group of authors together to help educate and amplify one another. And to these brilliant authors who were insanely generous in sharing their time and insights with me: Eve Rodsky, Susan McPherson, Fran Hauser, Reshma Saujani, Tiffany Dufu, and Julia Boorstin.

Lia, Fita, Nayeli, thank you for your incredible dedication to our family. Our house is forever simmering with new businesses, creative projects, recipe development, birthday parties, and playdates, and you keep it from boiling over! Thank you for caring so beautifully for our family and for allowing me the precious space and time I needed to write this book.

They say to surround yourself with people who lift you up, and I've got that covered. To my sisterhood: thank you for your friendship and for the many adventures—big and small—that keep my heart full. You all are the best lunch table pals a girl could ask for and you mean so much to me.

Thank you to my friends and early readers who helped me with edits, challenged me to dig just a little bit deeper, and helped push this book boulder up its mountain: Nancy Paul, Jenni Kayne, Meredith Kovach, Jane Buckingham, Emily Love, Sarah Tuff, Jordan Weinstock, and Daisy Goodman. And much gratitude to my spirit guides who lit a fire under me to write this book: Kasey Crown, Sasha Heinz, Cathy Heller, Susie Moore, and Nicole Whiting.

Thank you to Marcy Engelman, my longtime partner, friend, and champion. You are a force and I adore you. To Marissa Eigenbrood, Janet Shapiro, Courtney Link, and Rachel Fischer at Smith Publicity, thank you for your enthusiasm, professionalism, and hard work in launching this book to the world. Your team is amazing. Thank you to Stephanie Jucar for the thought leadership love and to Alice Dabell and Lindsay Mitrosilis for your essential social support!

INDEX

ABOUT THE AUTHOR

Candace Nelson is a serial entrepreneur, *New York Times* bestselling author, *Wall Street Journal* contributor, angel investor, TV personality, executive producer, and mom.

Candace worked in investment banking and then at an internet startup before shifting gears to follow her passion and attend pastry school. In 2005, she opened the doors to Sprinkles, the world's first cupcake bakery. Despite the early naysayers, her tiny bakery in Beverly Hills disrupted the legacy bakery industry and ignited a worldwide cupcake phenomenon. In 2012, Sprinkles introduced its Cupcake ATM, a cutting edge contactless cupcake delivery system. Today, Sprinkles has sold more than 200 million cupcakes and has more than twenty stores, thirty Cupcake ATMs, and a thousand employees.

In 2017, Candace cofounded Pizzana, a fast-growing chain of award-winning neo-Neapolitan pizzerias, leading the third wave of pizza in the US. Pizzana cemented Los Angeles as a pizza destination and revolutionized pizza takeout with its innovative heat-and-slice-at-home method. Pizzana also ships its frozen pizza nationwide. In 2021, Candace cocreated and executive produced *Best in Dough*, a Hulu show starring Pizzana Executive Chef Daniele Uditi.

Through CN2 Ventures, a family office and venture studio, Candace has backed a diverse portfolio of startups in the specialty food, retail, health, wellness, and early childhood spaces, with a focus on female and underrepresented founders.

Candace is also a beloved global baking personality. On the small screen, she starred in (and executive produced) Netflix's *Sugar Rush* and

Food Network's *Cupcake Wars*. She is also the author of the *New York Times* bestselling cookbook *The Sprinkles Baking Book*.

She lives in Los Angeles with her husband, Charles, her two sons, and her Norwich Terrier, Willy.

● ● ● ● ○

Follow her on Instagram and TikTok
@candacenelson